ARABIC
PROVERBS

ARABIC PROVERBS

JOHN LEWIS BURCKHARDT

DOVER PUBLICATIONS, INC.
MINEOLA, NEW YORK

Bibliographical Note

This Dover edition, first published in 2004, is an unabridged republication of *Arabic Proverbs; or The Manners and Customs of the Modern Egyptians, Illustrated from Their Proverbial Sayings Current at Cairo*, originally published by J. Murray, London, in 1830.

International Standard Book Number: 0-486-43436-2

Manufactured in the United States of America
Dover Publications, Inc., 31 East 2nd Street, Mineola, N.Y. 11501

TRANSLATOR'S PREFACE.

MANY of the proverbial sayings translated in this volume, were collected by *Sheref ed dýn Ibn Asad,* (شرف الدين ابن اسد) a native of Cairo, who lived, it is said, early in the last century, but never acquired a very high literary reputation. The translator found those Proverbs written upon nine or ten leaves in the common-place book of a sheikh, with whom he was acquainted in this city; but they wanted explanation or commentary. Of those he has omitted a considerable number, many being altogether uninteresting, and others so grossly indelicate that he could not venture to lay them before the public, although it must be acknowledged that they excelled in wit. Several sayings which appear to have been popular in the time of Ibn Asad, are no longer current; and these the translator has marked with an asterisk.

The original collection he has augmented by some hundreds, committed to paper as he heard them quoted in general society or in the bázár. Where the sense of a Proverb did not seem quite clear, he has explained it, or at least noticed the meaning commonly assigned to it, as well as any peculiarity of language wherever the provincial idiom differs from the learned Arabic. In this labour he was assisted by many intelligent Arabs of Cairo. The natives, in general, are so fond of figurative language and of witty allusions and comparisons taken from low life, that these sayings are constantly quoted on every common occasion, and express the tendency or moral of an event much better than could be done by a long or flowery speech. Many of these sayings are rhythmical, and sometimes the rhymes are extremely happy; but the drollery is lost in a plain translation, which has been rendered as literal as possible, and in which the true sense has never been sacrificed to elegance. They are written in the vulgar dialect of Cairo, such as every inhabitant understands and every one uses, except perhaps a few who affect to despise the language of the lower classes. These Proverbs offer a genuine specimen of the Arabic at present spoken in the Egyptian capital, and the same, or very nearly the same, as that used in the towns of the Delta.

These sayings are useful, as they serve to show us how the Arabs judge of men and things, and in this respect it must be acknowledged that many are dictated by wisdom and sagacity. Several Scriptural sayings and maxims of ancient sages will be found here naturalized among Arabs; as well as some

Proverbs which have generally been supposed of European origin.

Meidani has collected many sayings that were current among the ancient Arabs at the most brilliant period of their social state and of their language; but the present collection offers to our view a different nation and different manners; it also exhibits in some places an adulterated dialect, and alludes to vices which were probably but little known among the forefathers of the Egyptians. It proves, however, that the language is not by any means so corrupted as various travellers have imagined, and that the principles of virtue and honour, of friendship and true charity, of independence and generosity, are perfectly well known to the modern inhabitants of Egypt, although very few among them take the trouble of regulating their conduct accordingly.

The number of *nine hundred and ninety-nine* Proverbs might easily have been augmented by one, but the translator refrains from completing the thousand, adopting here a notion prevalent among Arabs, that even numbers are unlucky, and that any thing perfect in its quantity is particularly affected by the evil eye. He does not pretend to possess such a thorough knowledge of the learned Arabic as would have enabled him to indicate every instance of discrepancy between the language of these popular sayings and that used by the ancient Arabian writers. His long residence at Cairo rendered the vulgar idiom of its inhabitants familiar to him ; and knowing how few specimens of that idiom have hitherto been published, he flatters himself with the hope that this collection may interest and gratify the Orientalist, and that his explanations will be regarded as the hasty work of a traveller subject to numerous inconveniences, and who may, in some cases, have been deceived by erroneous or defective information, and not criticised as the elaborate treatise of a learned Arabic scholar or grammarian, surrounded by all the means of making his composition perfect.

CAIRO, 25th *of March*, 1817.

NOTE OF THE EDITOR.

To Burckhardt's short Preface a few lines must here be added. That accomplished traveller has sufficiently explained his motives for withholding from publication several Proverbs which had found a place in his original collection. It seems necessary that the Editor should account why this volume does not contain even so many as Burckhardt evidently intended to publish (nine hundred and ninety-nine). The numerical series is interrupted in various parts of the manuscript, not by any accidental injury, mutilation, or loss of leaves, but by chasms, which amount in some instances to whole decades of Proverbs; the most considerable deficiency occurring where (in the middle of a page) immediately after No. 516 follows No. 577. These omissions may not unreasonably be supposed to have arisen from the writer's mistake of one figure for another; in fact the 1 of No. 516 so much resembles a 7, (being nearly joined to the 5 by a stroke of the pen at its upper part,) that it might easily deceive the eye. Some allowance must also be made for the effect of those inconvenient circumstances to which our ingenious traveller has above alluded. Under whatever circumstances of difficulty, danger, or inconvenience, he may have collected and explained these Proverbs, his work offers a variety of curious and original information respecting the manners, customs, and opinions of an extraordinary people; while his philological remarks must prove highly useful and interesting to all who are desirous of understanding, with critical accuracy, the modern Arabic dialect used at Cairo.

In the composition of this work, as of his volumes already published, he adopted the language of our country, and generally with sufficient correctness; it has been, however, in some places, necessary to substitute an English for a foreign idiom, Burckhardt's meaning being on all occasions most scrupulously preserved; even where his translation of certain terms or phrases (which the Arabic scholar will soon discover) appeared more literal than decent, it has been endeavoured by circumlocution to express the sense without offending delicacy. These and the omission of a few Proverbs (found to agree most exactly both in words and signification with others given under preceding numbers) constitute the only liberties which have been assumed by the Editor.

WILLIAM OUSELEY.

London, May 21st, 1830.

ERRATUM.—Proverb No. 138. *For* صابت *read* صاحت

ARABIC PROVERBS

OF THE

MODERN EGYPTIANS.

حرف الالف

No. 1.

الف دقدق ولا سلام عليك

A thousand raps at the door, but no salute or invitation from within.

This is said of a person's fruitless endeavours to become intimate with another.

2.

الف تغا ولا تغاي

(Let them strike or slap) a thousand necks, but not mine.

Among the Arabs it is usual to strike the neck (تغا) and not the ears. A blow on the neck is con-

sidered a much greater affront than a slap on the
face. Not only the neck, but a blow struck upon
the neck, is expressed in the Egyptian dialect by تفا.
Thus "I struck him a blow on his neck," (ضربته تفا)
is exactly equivalent in its meaning to the English
phrase, "I boxed his ears."

3.

الف كركي في اجوّ ما تعوض عصفور في الكف

*A thousand cranes in the air are not worth one
sparrow in the fist.*

The crane كركي is a bird common in the Delta,
particularly about the Lake of Menzaleh. كف properly signifies the "hand," or "palm of the hand;"
but in Egypt is generally used for the "fist."

4.

اذا كان القمر معك لا تبالي بالنجوم

*If the moon be with thee, thou needest not to care
about the stars.*

5.

اذا كان معك نحس لا تسيبه يجيك انحس منه

*If a worthless fellow be with thee, do not let him go, or
else one worse will come to thee.*

The general meaning is, that we should bear
present ills rather than, by endeavouring to remove
them, expose ourselves to greater. This saying

is often quoted with respect to servants, whose dishonesty and insolence are subjects of universal complaint throughout Egypt. The word يسيب in common acceptation signifies "to leave a thing, to let it go out of one's hands." The word نحس is used in Egypt to express a low, disorderly, unprincipled character—a base, worthless fellow.

6.

اذا كانت العمايم تشتكي الفسة ايش يكون حال الألبسة

If the turbans complain of a slight wind, what must be the state of the inner drawers?

This proverb is quoted when the citizens of Cairo murmur at oppression, the peasants having much greater reason for being discontented. الفسة flatus, البسة—اي شي in ايش in the Egyptian dialect used for plural of لباس, drawers worn under the great trowsers.

7.

اذا كان زوجي راضي ايش فضول القاضي

If my husband consent, why should the kadhy's inter-ference be necessary.

This means in general that when two parties who have contended agree to be reconciled, the arbitration of a third person is not requisite. But the saying more particularly alludes to divorces, which in many cases are determined by the kadhy. فضول in the Egyptian dialect, signifies—the meddling, officious interference of a third person.

8.

اذا نسيت الحمد تصلّي بايش

*If thou forgettest to say " Praise be to God," in what
other words wilt thou pray?*

This is addressed to persons who neglect the
principal object, or part of their business, and execute
only that which is the least important.   الحمد means
the expression الحمد لله, which commences the *Fateha*,
or first chapter of the Koran, and should be recited
in every prayer.   بايش in the Egyptian dialect for
باي شي.   The Egyptians always put this after the
verb in interrogations, as تصلّي بايش—whilst the
Syrians invariably place it before, and say بايش تصلّي.

9.

اذا كرهك جارك غيّر باب دارك

*If thy neighbour dislike thee, change the gate of thy
house.*

The intimacy with neighbours is much greater in
the East than in Europe ; and the repose of a family
often depends upon the harmony subsisting between
it and those who occupy the adjoining house.

10.

اذا حلق جارك بل انت

*If thy neighbour shaves (somebody), do thou soak (the
head of the person whom he shaves).*

Always endeavour to act agreeably to the wishes

of thy neighbour. يبل to wet, meaning here to wet
the head with a lather of soap before the application
of a razor.

11.

اذا اراد ربنا هلاك نملة انبت لها اجنحة

*If God proposes the destruction of an ant, he allows
wings to grow upon her.*

The sudden elevation of persons to stations above
their means or capacities, may often cause their ruin.

12.

اذا رايت اعور عبر اقلب حجر

*If thou seest a one-eyed person pass by, turn up a
stone.*

The people of Cairo turn up a stone or break a
water-jar behind the back of any person whom they
dislike, just on his leaving them, hoping thereby to
prevent his return; this is a kind of incantation.
The term *one-eyed* here expresses a person disagreeable on any account. The Arabs regard a one-eyed
man as of bad omen (شُوم), and nobody wishes to
meet him.

13.

اذا رايت حيط مايل هرول من تحتها

If thou seest a wall inclining, run from under it.

Fly from him whose power is tottering, or whom
dangers threaten. In the Egyptian dialect حيط is
used for حايط.

14.

اذا كثرت الالوان اعرّف انها من بيوت الجيران

If the dishes increase in number, it becomes known that they are from the houses of neighbours.

In the East, neighbours frequently supply the wants of their friend's kitchen on occasion of family feasts. This saying implies that when a person makes too expensive an entertainment, it is evident that he has borrowed from others. لون (in the plural الوان) means not only "a colour," but, among the Egyptians, a dish of dressed victuals.

15.

اذا كترت النواتية غرقت الركب

If the sailors become too numerous, the ship sinks.

كترت instead of كثرت. The ث is seldom pronounced in Egypt.

16.

اذا حبتك حية اطوق بها

If a serpent love thee, wear him as a necklace.

If dangerous people show affection towards thee, court their friendship by the most polite attention.

17.

اذا انكسر التجمل حمّل حمل حمار

If thy camel break down, put on an ass-load.

Suit thy business to thy circumstances.

18.

اذا كان الكفن مخلّق و الغاسل اعور و الدكة مكسورة و الارض سباخة
يكون الميّت من اهل جهنم

*If the winding-sheet be ragged, and the corpse-washer
one-eyed, and the bier broken, and the burial-
ground a saltish soil, then truly the deceased
must belong to the inhabitants of hell.*

If everything in a person's business goes wrong,
he must be totally ruined at last. دكة is properly a
stand or frame on which the coffin rests before it is
removed to the grave.

19.

اذا بُليت بالشحاتة دقّ الابواب الكبار

*If mendicity should unfortunately be thy lot, knock at
the large gates only.*

Ask assistance from those only who have the
power of helping thee.

20.

اذا كان البصل يُهلّل له فالسكر ايش نقول له

*If an onion causes his loud rejoicings, what then shall
we say to sugar?*

Said of people who bestow admiration upon trifling
objects.

21.

اذا سموك حصاد شرشر منجلك

If they call thee reaper, whet thy scythe.

Endeavour, even by mere appearances, to convince people that thou deservest the reputation that thou enjoyest.

22.

اذا حضر الماأ بطل التيمّم

If water is present for ablution, the use of sand is discontinued.

Affluence renders unnecessary what is practised during poverty. التيمّم is the ablution with sand which the Turkish law prescribes when water cannot be procured.

23.

اذا حضرت الملايكة غابت الشياطين

When the angels present themselves, the devils abscond.

24.

اذا هبّ الهوي دخل دخل الشقوق

If the wind blows, it enters at every crevice.

A lucky person is fortunate in the most trifling affair. شقوق plural of شتى, a fissure in the wall.

25.

اذا كان في اِيدك دهن دهن امسحه فن اقرب الناس اليك

If there be grease on thy hand, rub it off at thy nearest friend's.

Let your own kindred, and not strangers, share in your superfluities, or the fragments from your table. ‏ايد‎ is used at Cairo for ‏يد‎—and pronounced there *eed*, not *yed*, as it ought to be.

26.

‏اذا رايته يسبّه اعلم انه يحبّه‎

If thou seest him reproaching and swearing at him,
know that he loves him.

De amatoribus dicitur. ‏سبّ‎ is commonly used at Cairo for reviling, calling opprobrious names, or swearing at a person.

27.*

‏اذا جا الماء طوفان اجعل ابنك تحت رجليك‎

If the water come like a deluge, place thy son under
thy feet.

Save thyself, even at the expense of thy nearest kindred or friends—a selfish principle very general in the Levant. According to Moslim tradition, when the deluge came and the rebel sons of Noah felt the water approach their ankles, they took their little children in their arms; when the water rose higher, they placed them upon their shoulders, then upon their heads; but at last, when the flood reached to their own mouths, they put the children under their feet, endeavouring to keep their own heads above the water.

28.*

‏اللص العيار ما يسرق من حارته شيء‎

The thief who understands his business does not steal
from his own quarter (of the town).

‏العيار‎, able, clever, expert.

29.

اخر الليل تسمع العياط

At the close of the night the cries are heard.

This saying is addressed to persons exulting in
good fortune, to warn them of the final issue The
night may have passed tranquilly, but at the end
affrays often happen, occasioned either by drunkards,
profligates coming from the houses of public women,
or by robbers, who generally commit depredations at
that time, when they suppose the inhabitants to be
asleep.

30.

اخر الطب الكي

The ultimate remedy is a cautery.

If nothing else will avail, violent measures must
be at last adopted.

31.

العرس عرس ابونا و الناس يضاربونا

*The nuptials are the nuptials of our father, yet the
people fight with us.*

Those who have the strongest claim find themselves dispossessed of the advantage by others. This
saying alludes to a crowd of fellows who have assembled at a nuptial entertainment, but beat and
displace the bridegroom's children, to make room for
themselves.

32.

الحبلة الشتهته و المرضعة اكلته

The pregnant woman longed for it, but the nurse ate it.

This proverb resembles in sense that immediately preceding. The whims of pregnant women are treated with indulgence in the East as well as in Europe.

33.

الطحّان ياخد كف بكف و ربّنا ياخد بغل ببغل

*The miller takes (steals) handful by handful, but the
Lord takes (sums up his reckoning) mule (load)
by mule (load).*

ياخد in Egypt used for ياخذ—the ذ being generally pronounced as د.

34.

الحجامة بالغاس و لا الحاجة لناس

*Rather be scarified with an axe than require favours
from others.*

الحاجة for الاحتياج. It might likewise mean a thing, or شي (as hereafter remarked), and so understood would signify, "better to be scarified with an axe than to owe or be indebted to others for anything." الحجامة means *cupping*, also to make mere scarifications on the forehead or legs—a common practice in the Levant. Among the Bedouins, a father threatening his son, says, اذا فعلته نحجمك "if you do so we shall cup (or scarify) you."

35.

الريّس يحبّك امسح يدك في القلع

*The captain (of the ship) loves thee, wipe thy hand
on the sail.*

He who is favoured by government may do any
thing with impunity.

36.

انا احب حماتي و احب عند انفي تغسي

*(Yes)—I like my mother-in-law, and I like also that
she should make a (disgusting) smell under my
nose (crepitum reddendo).*

This refers to a silly, obstinate fellow, who per-
sists in longing for what offends others. In the East
it is generally supposed that a mother-in-law cannot
long be on good terms with the son-in-law, and her
name is commonly used as a term expressing "disagreeable kindred." Here is to be understood
احب انها عند

37.*

العب مع العبد يوريك شقه

Play with a slave, he will show to thee his hinder parts.

Low people become insolent if you admit them to
familiarity. شق is equivalent to طيز—or rather to
خرق الطيز

38.

اعور وقعت في عينه الصاحيحة قشّة قال الله
يمسيكم بالخير

*A splinter entered the sound eye of a one-eyed person.
" I wish you good night," said he.*

He fancied that night had arrived. This refers
to those who judge the world merely by their own
sensations, and suppose that every one must feel as
they do. قَشّة in the Egyptian dialect, signifies any
small piece of wood, straw, &c.

39.*

احدب و يشَقلَب

He is hump-backed, yet whirls about.

يشقلب properly expresses those " tours de force "
practised by a rope dancer in wheeling round his
whole body with the head forwards.

40.

اعمي و يشالق

He is blind, and still ogles the women.

يتشالق or يشالق علي النسوان is commonly used at
Cairo to describe the glances which a man passing in
the street directs towards the shutters, behind which
the women sit.

41.*

الكلام لك يا جارة الا انت حمارة

*It is to thee I speak, my (fair) neighbour; but truly
thou art an ass.*

This is said of dull persons, unable to comprehend
a slight hint.   A man conversing with his own wife,
was desirous of giving a hint to his neighbour's wife,
of whom he was the gallant, and who overheard the
conversation; but she did not understand him, and
he in a rage used the words above quoted.

42.

ان جات الدادة احنّ من الوالدة دي حنية فاسدة

*If the midwife happen to have more commiseration
(for the child) than the mother, that is a corrupt
feeling.*

The humane intentions of inferior officers are of
little avail, if the spirit of government be unmerciful.
الدادة the midwife.   دي used in Egypt for هذي.
حنية may likewise be translated " affection."

43.*

ايش ما طبّخت العمشة لزوجها بيتعشا

*Whatever the half-blind wife cooks for her husband,
he sups on it.*

Custom reconciles us to bad living.   عمش half-blind, sore-eyed. (The Egyptians frequently use the imprecation, "*blindness to thy eyes*," عَش في عينك.) The ب of بيتعشا is according to the Egyptian dialect, and often prefixed to verbs; but still more commonly in Syria than in Egypt.

44*.

اللي في الدِست تطلَعه المِغرفة

What is in the cauldron is taken out with the kitchen spoon.

Every affair requires its own peculiar treatment, and its own people to bring it to a conclusion : also, to obtain information, the proper mode must be adopted. اللي used in Egypt for الذي. يطلع has many significations; it here means "to take out." المِغرفة is the great kitchen ladle or wooden spoon.

45.

الباطل ما له رجلين

The lazy person has no legs.

The Egyptians pronounce لَه as if it were written لُو *loo*, instead of saying *lahoo*.

46.

الجِنازة حامية والمِيت كلب

The burial is attended by crowds of people, the deceased is—a dog.

Alluding to great honours bestowed on persons not worthy of them. حامية signifies a burial or funeral when it is "hot ;" i.e., attended by multitudes.

47.

العب بالمقصوص حتي يجيك الديواني

Play with false coin until thou gettest a díwány.

مقصوص is the old clipped silver or copper coin,
likewise false coin. The Egyptians more generally
use زغل or زيوف to express false money. *Díwány* is
the same as *párá.* To gain, begin humbly.

48.

الفرخ الناجب من البيضة يبان

The fine pullet shows its excellence from the egg.

The pullets most likely to thrive are those which
cry from the very egg. This is likewise expressed
by the saying

الكتكوت الناصح من البيضة يصيح

The words فرخ and كتكوت are synonymous.

49.*

الدنيا مراية اوريها توريك

*The world is a mirror; show thyself in it, and it will
reflect thy image.*

We may also translate thus : " show thyself in it
(i.e., be frank with the people), and it will let thee
see its image " (i.e., people will be frank with thee).
This meaning would be more clearly expressed by
the words اوريها نفسك توريك نفسها. In the Egyptian
dialect مراية is used for مرأة.

50.

الليلة النيّرة من العصر بيّنة

From the aszer (or afternoon) it appears whether the night will be clear.

This (like No. 48) means that a person gives indications of his future virtues from early youth. بيّنة is much used among the Egyptians for باينة.

51.

اتعمّم بأسفوط ولا تنسي الشروط

Tie a turban of straw round thy head, but do not forget thy engagements.

Play the fool as much as thou wilt, but observe thy promises and engagements. اسفوط ribbands of straw from which baskets are made. Idiots fasten them like turbans about their heads. يتعمّم signifies "to tie a turban."

52.

المستعجل و البطي عند المعديّة يلتقي

The hasty and the tardy meet at the ferry.

Extremes often meet: معديّة a ferry-boat. The ferries wait a long time on the banks of the Nile, until the complement of passengers be full.

53.

الاسم لطوبة و الفعايل لمشير

Tooba bears the name, but the deeds belong to Emshyr.

This alludes to the common saying, برد طوبة "the cold of the Tooba," which in Egypt is applied to any considerable degree of cold. Tooba is the Coptic month comprehending the greater part of January : but the coldest month in Egypt, although it has not the character of being so, is Emshyr, the month next after Tooba.

54.

اشتهينا علي دي الطَلَقَ يجي غلام

From the mother's efforts in labour, we expected the birth of a male child.

" Parturiunt montes, nascitur ridiculus mus." Sons are much more desired than daughters throughout the East.   طلتي   "the labour of a woman in child-bed."

55.*

اعمل بحبّة و حاسب البطّال

Work (were it only) for a single grain, and reckon up the profits of him who does nothing.

حبّة often means "a trifle." Thus it is said, و لا حبّة "not even the smallest trifle."

56.

ان لقيتها قطع ايزارها قال الدورة علي لمّ الشمل

If thou find her, cut her veil in two. "The object is now to find the chance of meeting her," he replied.

It is not sufficient to form projects, circumstances must favour us in executing them.   ايزار a woman's veil, generally of black silk or cotton.   قال is here put for القايل قال. In the Egyptian dialect دورة means "now, for once, above all." دورتي "in my turn." لم الشمل literally, "the gathering together what is separated;" or as here, "to cause or find a meeting." The expression الدورة علي لم الشمل often signifies nothing more than "if, if!"

57.

انا اخبر بشمس بلدي

I best know the sun of my own country.

Every one knows best his own affairs, and those interested in them.

58.

الزلابية محرّمة علي الكلاب

The Zalabye is (a dish) forbidden to the dogs.[1]

The higher classes only can enjoy certain pleasures. زلابية are round cakes. made of flour, butter, and sugar; not much in fashion of late at Cairo.

59.*

المحتاج اخو القرنان

The needy is the brother of the cuckold.

The needy husband connives at the dishonourable earnings of his unfaithful wife. The term قرنان (cuckold) is no longer used at Cairo. Cuckolds and procurers are generally comprised under the same appellation معرس, which is the common expression of insult among the Egyptians, and heard on every occasion. Equivalent to معرس are the words قرواد and دماغ.

60.

الَّخُنْفِسَة في عين امها مليحَة

The beetle is a beauty in the eyes of its mother.

On the infatuation of parents. The beetle
(خنفسة) is cited by the present Egyptians as remarkable for its ugliness. They use مليح in the sense
of "handsome."

61.

العمل بالزيت و لا القعاد في البيت

*Work, though thy gain be merely the oil, rather than
sit (idle) at home.*

This alludes to the oil with which lamps are
lighted, and which costs each family at least two
paras every night. To express that a man is
reduced to abject poverty, the Egyptians say, "he
has not as much as would pay for the oil." ما عنده
حق الزيت

62.

الفايدة في الخرا و لا الغرامة في المسك

Gain upon dirt rather than loss upon musk.

Endeavour to gain in low pursuits rather than
lose in brilliant concerns. غرامة is used in Egypt to
signify "loss;" but the term خسارة is more frequently employed.

63.

ان سلمت الدار من سعيد ماجي احد من بعيد

If the house be relieved from (the presence of) Sayd,
no other will come from afar.

This relates in general to importunate and intruding visitors. Sayd was one of those parasites (called طفيل) who in former times were established as a regular corporation at Cairo, and became a plague to all who gave entertainments. They have their chief or sheikh, and obtruded their company at every private feast, unless they were induced by a present to depart from the house.

64.

العاقل من غمزة والمجنون من لكزة

The wise with a wink, the fool with a kick (are taught
to understand).

65.

اتبع البوم يودّيك الخراب

Follow the owl, she will lead thee to a ruined place.

On the consequences of bad company. يودّي in constant use among the Egyptians, signifying "to carry," "to lead," "to transport."

66.

الدبّان يعرف وجه اللبّان

The fly knows the face of the milk-seller.

This proverb chiefly refers to the dancing girls,

who, when they are brought for the amusement of
company, pay attention particularly to those whom
they soon discover to be the most inclined towards
them.

67.

ابليس ما يخرب بيته

The devil does not destroy his (own) house.

68.

ابليس يعرف ربّه لكن يتخابت

The devil knows his Lord, but still practises evil.

On a person who understands the precepts of
religion, but never acts according to them.   In the
Egyptian dialect, يتخابت for يتخابث "to practise
foul deeds," "to intrigue," or "embroil."

69.

السلطان ينشتم في غيبته

The Sultan is reviled in his absence (only).

70.

البيت لنا و الحديت لنا

To us belong the house, and the talking (therein).

This expresses that we are here sole masters, or
that it is our own affair exclusively.   حديت for
حديث.

71.*

القحبة الجوادة ما تريد لها قوادة

*The public woman who is liberal (of her favours), does
not wish for a procuress.*

A thorough scoundrel wants no inducement to
bad actions. قوادة a procuress. قحبة commonly used
in Egypt for an unchaste female or prostitute.

72.*

اهل العرس يشتهوا المرق

The people concerned in the nuptials long for the broth.

Those nearest to wealth are often prevented from
enjoying it; the great enjoy the least. In this proverb it is supposed that the guests devour all the
meat of the nuptial feast, leaving the members of
the family to long even for the broth.

73.

اخلط الهم بالزبيبة

Mingle thy sorrow with Zebybe.

Drown your griefs in pleasures. زبيبة is a pre-
paration from the flower of hemp, opium, and honey,
excessively intoxicating. It is used among the lower
classes and peasants. In Hedjaz this flower of hemp
is mixed with raisins (called *Zebyb*) and tobacco, and
is smoked in the Persian pipe; from which mixture
the name of Zebybe has probably been derived.

74.

اما بالجمل او بالجمّال او بصاحب الجمل

(*The misfortune*) *falls either upon the camel, or upon
the camel-driver, or upon the owner of the camel.*

This expresses that if a person be once unlucky,
he is unfortunate in every thing, whether with
respect to his family or his business.

75.*

اوقد شمعة وفتش جمعة تلتقي شي قدر الودعة

*Light a candle; search for a whole week; thou wilt
find something worth a shell.*

On fruitless or childish exertions. ودعة are small
white shells brought from the Red Sea, which serve
as playthings for children, and as counters in the
game of mangal. تلتقي used in Egypt for تلقي

76.*

العصفور يتغلّي و الصياد يتقلّي

*The little bird picks its breast, while the sportsman
sets his net.*

The word عصفور , properly a sparrow, is often
used to express any small bird. يتغلّي in the original
sense means to pick the vermin off the head or body
of a child. The birds in performing that operation
upon themselves always appear to be much pleased.
In Egypt it is said of a person عمال يتغلّي to express
that he is in a thoughtless state of security or happy
leisure. (عمال) stands for يعمل "he does;" and is an

auxiliary verb in constant use.) يَتَقَلَّى properly signifying " to fry a piece of meat in the pan ;" here
means, " to turn the ends of the net-strings in the
sportsman's hand, as meat is turned with a spoon in
the frying-pan."

77.*

الوحدة و لا القرين السو

To live single rather than have ill-natured companions.

78.*

احتاجوا لليهودي قال اليوم عيدي

*They stood in need of the Jew (to assist thèm)—this
day, said he, is my feast-day.*

Addressed to persons unwilling to serve or oblige.

79.*

الف عشيق و لا مستحل

A thousand lovers rather than one Mostahel.

Many lovers or gallants cause less shame to a
woman than one *Mostahel.* According to the Moslim
law a person who has once divorced his wife cannot
re-marry her, until she has been married to some
other man who becomes her legitimate husband,
cohabits with her for one night, and divorces her the
next morning ; after which the first husband may
again possess her as his wife. Such cases are of
frequent occurrence—as men in the haste of anger
often divorce their wives by the simple expression

طلقتك—which cannot be retracted. In order to
regain his wife a man hires (at no inconsiderable
rate) some peasant, whom he chooses from the ugliest
that can be found in the streets; but who must
engage effectually to consummate the nuptials. A
temporary husband of this kind is called *Mostahel*,
and is generally most disgusting to the wife.

80.

اللي تجمعه النملة في سنة تاكله الغارة في ليلة

What the ant collects in the course of a whole year,
the monk eats up in one night.

الذي for اللي

81.

ايش تبالي السما بعياط الكلاب

What does heaven care for the cries of the dogs?

On the indifference of government to the complaints of the lower classes. يبال "to care for"
—"be attentive to:" thus it is said, دير بالك "take
care."

82.*

اقلّ الزاد يوصل البلاد

The smallest stock of provisions supports (the traveller
back) to his home.

البلاد is often employed, as here, for one's home
or country.

83.

لسرّ معه في بيت الوالي

A secret confided to him may be regarded as if it were (published) in the house of the police officers.

الوالي is the chief officer of police, in whose house every private transaction becomes known.

84.

اعطاه من الشاة ودنها

He gave him the sheep's ear (for his share).

This relates to unjust or unequal divisions. ودن is used in Egypt for اذن

85.

اسقاه الخلّ باجنحة الدبّان

He gave him the vinegar to drink upon the wings of flies.

He devised the most artful and ignominious methods of slowly tormenting him.

86.

اوراه النجوم بالنهار

He let him see the stars in day-time.

This proverb is exclusively applied to those who from stinginess keep their own people in such a state of hunger that they become faint, and every object seems black to their eyes.

87.

ارقص للقرد في دولته

When the monkey reigns, dance before him.

88.

الريس في حساب و النوتي في حساب

The captain (of the ship) means one way, the sailor another.

Of a person who gives such an answer as does not relate to the question asked. حساب is not used here in its usual sense, of "account," but stands for نية or "meaning." Thus it is said حسبت اني اروح هناك "I meant to go there."

89.

اردب ما هو لك لا تحضر كيله تتغبّر دقنك و تتعب في شيله

If the erdeb (of corn) does not belong to thee, be not present when it is measured out; (else) thy beard will be dusted, and thou wilt be wearied with the removing of it.

Do not trouble thyself about the business of others, else thou wilt repent it. اردب the Egyptian corn-measure, equal to about fifteen bushels.

90.

الفرّاش الشاطر ما يحتاج مهماز

The clever and active valet wants no one to set him right.

The lazy only require spurs. الفرّاش in Egypt

signifies the valet de chambre, who keeps his master's clothes and keys, is the chief among his servants, and generally his confidant. The Egyptians use the word مهماز to express a man who is lazy himself and only occupied in the affairs of others. The Moggrebyns give this name to " spurs." In Egypt شاطر denotes one who is both active and clever in his business.

91.

العزالة الشاطرة تغزل برجل حمار

A clever spinster spins with an ass's foot (as her distaff).

Of those who do much with small means.

92.

الحيطان لها ودان

The walls have ears.

ودان for ودان

93.

الداخل بين البصلت و قشرتها ما يخرج الا بصنتها

He who introduces himself between the onion and the peel, does not go forth without its strong smell.

On the consequences of intimacy with bad people. صنة is used in Egypt for " stink " or " bad smell."

94.

المصارين في البطن يضاربوا

(Even) the entrails in the belly quarrel together.

On family broils.

95.

اطعم الفم تستحي العين

Feed the mouth, the eye will be bashful.

Give presents to great people and they will be ashamed not to look upon you with kindness. This saying is very common at Cairo.

96.

ابيع من اخوة يوسف

*He sells his friend more easily than the brethren of
Joseph sold him.*

البايع signifies at Cairo one who abandons his old friends for new, on the slightest prospect of gain. The history of Joseph is very finely told in the Korán.

97.

اطمع من اشعب

(He is) more greedy than Ashab.

98.

اكذب من مُسَيْلَمَة

A greater liar than Moseylama.

These two sayings relate to Ashab and Moseylama, ancient Arabs (the latter a false prophet)

remarkable for the vices here imputed to them.
These personages are noticed in the following fine
verses :—

و وعدتني حتي حسبتك صادقا

فجعلت من طمع اجيه و اذهب

فاذا حضرت انا و انت بمجلس

قالوا مسيلمة و هذا اشعب

Thou gavest me thy pledge so that I believed it to be true
In my greedy hopes I went (to thy abode) and turned back
If in society thou and I should meet,
People will say, "here is Moseylama—and that is Ashab.

99.

اتبع الكذاب لباب الدار

Follow the liar to the gate of his house.

To ascertain whether he has spoken truth. لباب
used in Egypt for الي باب

100.*

ايش يبالي البطاح اذا خرب المراح

What does the wolf care if the sheep-fold be destroyed?

بطاح the same as ذيب—a wolf.

101.

الغَنْدَرَة المخفية التكه و الطاقية

Gay or expensive fashions (adopted but) concealed
consist in the Tikke and the Tákye.

Said of hypocrites or timid persons who declaim

against gay fashions, but secretly indulge in them.
El Tikke is a sash of silk or muslin, often embroidered,
with which the trowsers of men and women are
closely tied about the loins, while it remains hidden
under the garments. *El Tákye* signifies a white
cambric bonnet or cap, frequently embroidered, that
is worn close to the head under the red bonnet or
Tarbosh. In the Egyptian dialect الغندرة means
" high gaiety," " fashion," " liberality," " heartiness,"
" jollity." The words غندور and غندورة are very
common ; being applied also to low people, who in
their station and among their own acquaintances
affect to be smart and dashing. Those who do not
wish or who fear to make themselves too conspicuous
by an open display of gay fashions, console themselves
by having these two hidden articles of costly materials
and expensive workmanship. Both the *Tikke* and
the *Tákye* are among the first tokens of affection
sent by a lady to her lover. The *Tikke* affords
subject for many jokes in gay conversation.

102.

ايش افتكر لك يا بصلة مع كل عضة دمعة

*What can I think of thy good qualities, O onion! as
every bite draws tears?*

Said of men who in this respect are like the
onion. Here is to be understood,

ايش افتكر لك يا بصلة من المحاسن

and مع stands for مع انه

103.

راوا سكران يقرا قالوا له غنّي تشاكل بعضك

*They saw a drunkard reading (the Koran). Sing,
they said, and both thy occupations will resemble
each other.*

If the verb يقرا stand by itself, it is often to be
understood as يقرا القران

104.

ان طلعتِ حرّة علقي في ودني جرّة

*If thou shouldest prove a virtuous woman, hang a jar
on my ear.*

I shall submit to pain and ridicule if the woman
continue virtuous. حرّة virtuous, " as becomes a
free-born woman."

105.

العبد امّا اولته او اخرته

(Of) the slave (take) either the first or the last.

Beware of the pains that must be taken with a
half-bred man. Purchase the slave either when he
is quite young and raw, so that he may be educated
as you please ; or when he is full grown and all his
good or bad qualities can be discovered.

106.

اشتريناه للجباسة طلع للطاحون

*We bought him (the jackass) to turn the plaster (of
Paris) mill; but he proved fit only for the corn mill.*

On disappointed expectations. جبش gypsum, or

plaster of Paris. It requires much greater strength to turn the heavy gypsum mill, than a common corn mill. Almost every respectable house at Cairo has its own mill which is worked by a jackass.

107.

اسم بلا جسم

A name without a body (or reality).

This is said of persons who bear honourable names. Such as مصطفى—مالح—عبدالله—احمد—حسن —&c., but whose characters little answer to their names.

108.

السَّلَفَ تَلَفَ

Lending is ruinous (to lenders and borrowers).

There is a similar proverb :—

السّلفة تربّي العداوة

Lending nurses enmity.

سَلَفَ in the Egyptian dialect, " to advance or lend money."

109.

اعمل انت يا شقي لهذا المتّكي

Work thou, O unfortunate person, for this idle Sybarite.

المتكي one who sits at ease reclining upon his cushions; and, in general, the idle who enjoy every luxury.

110.

ام الجبان ما تحزن

The mother of the coward does not grieve (for him).

She has no cause to grieve for one who never exposes himself to danger.

111.

ان تابت القحبه عرصت

If the harlot repent, she becomes a procuress.

Similar to this proverb is the following :—

قحبة و هي صغيرة قوادة و هي كبيرة

112.

انت مغسّل و ضامن جنة

Thou art but the washerman (of the dead), yet thou wilt insure (him) Paradise.

On the airs of patronage or protection assumed by those who possess not any influence or authority whatever.

113.

ان جا الورد اكلنا و شربنا عليه و ان راح لا نتاسف عليه

If the rose come, we eat and drink near it; if it depart, we do not regret it.

We court the friendship of those whom we afterwards leave with indifference. This proverb alludes to the Eastern custom of having feasts and collations in gardens during the season of roses. عليه is here for عنده

114.

الآب عاشق و الام غيرانة و بنتهم في الدار حيرانة

*The father is a lover (of some one not in his own
house)—the mother is jealous—the daughter at
home is puzzled how to act.*

115.

الله لا يجعل لنا جار و له عينين

God grant us not any neighbour with-two eyes.

It is better that our neighbours should be half-
blind.

116.

ايش يبالي مَن يسرق الحمير اذا باع كل حمار بدرهم

*He who steals the asses, what does he care about
selling each of them even for one derhem?*

117.*

الحرّ حرّ و لو مسّه الضّر

*An honourable man is honourable, even though mishaps
should befall him.*

حرّ signifies here " virtuous," or " honourable," as
above (in No. 104). Of this proverb the pronunciation at Cairo is as follows :—

> *El horr horr*
> *Wa low messoo eddorr,*

the *ow* in *low* having the sound of *ow* in the English
word *owl*.

118.*

المفرّط اولي بالخسارة

The inconsiderate is the first to lose (or nearest to loss).

Some robbers attacked a house, and the owner was forced to give them a hundred pieces of coin ; but these being all base money, the robbers were detected in the bázár, where they went to make purchases. One of them on his way to the scaffold, passed by the house of the person robbed, and reproached him for his cunning ; but the man replied, انت المفرّط " thou art the inconsiderate person :" which words gave origin to this proverb. There is a common phrase at Cairo, فرطت في الشي الفلانه "I have foolishly or inconsiderately lost such a thing." The people of Upper Egypt use the word ودر in the same sense—thus, انا ودرت الشي—this is probably a corruption of the verb يذر or ودر.

119.*

اللسان عدو القفا

The tongue is the neck's enemy.

Bad language is retorted upon the neck of him who uses it, with a blow.

120.

التصبر علي الحبيب و لا فقده

To have patience with a friend rather than lose him for ever.

In the dialect of Cairo many terms are used in

the sense of "friend." صاحب denotes the first class
of friends—then follows حبيب or محب—and the
superlative is صديق.

121.

الحبل علي النجرّارة

To haul the rope is incumbent upon the boatmen.

Every one has, and should know, his own
business. Here is to be understood الحبل ذهبه علي
النجرّارة—The word الحبل is the rope by which boats
are dragged along the shore of the Nile against the
stream. النجرّارة are the boatmen who pull the rope,
or peasants hired for that purpose.

122.

القمح يدور و يجي الطاحون

*The corn passes from hand to hand, but comes at last
to the mill.*

However he may turn or shift, he will at last be
caught or fall into the hands of his enemy.

123.

ارميه البحر يطلع و في فمه سمكة

*Throw him into the river and he will rise with a fish
in his mouth.*

Said of a lucky or highly fortunate person. البحر
is here put for في البحر The term بحر expresses
throughout all Egypt the Nile or بحر النيل The

ة often added to nouns (as in سكة) not only marks
the feminine gender, but shows precisely that the
noun is singular—thus بقرة a single cow, طيرة a single
bird; but in common conversation the ة is frequently
added without any particular meaning.

124.*

اسلفه و العب معه تخسر معه

*Advance or lend him (money), and play or joke with
him; thou wilt lose by him.*

Jocularity with a debtor often causes the loss of
the money due.

125.

اعلح النية و نام في البرية

*Improve or correct thy intentions (preserve a clear
conscience) and sleep (without fear) in the desert.*

126.

اشتري بدرهم بلح ءادله في الحيّ نخل

*He bought for one derhem some dates; and has now
his palm-trees in the village.*

Said of boasters—this man wishes others to
believe that the dates which he purchased were the
produce of his own trees. In Egypt it is generally
considered by the peasants as an honour to possess
date trees, because they mostly belong to ancient

families and cannot easily be purchased. Of similar
meaning is the proverb :—

صاحب قراة في الفرس يركب

Let him who owns one kerát of the mare, mount her.

Fine horses and valuable mares are shared among
different proprietors, each of whom possesses a certain
number of the twenty-four *keráts* into which the
animal is supposed to be divided.

127.*

الدين سواد الخدّين

Debts cause both cheeks to become black.

Debts are a constant shame. سواد الانخد or سواد الوجه
is the distinguishing colour of wicked persons on the
(Moslim) Day of Judgment. In common discourse
it means "shame." The father says to his son, or
the friend to his companion, لا تسوّد وجهي "do not
blacken my face"—"do not let thy behaviour prove
a cause of shame to me."

128.

اوقع من الدبّان في العسل

*He falls more frequently (or more easily) than flies
fall into honey.*

اوقع is here used as the comparative of وقع an
irregular form often employed by the Egyptians. It
is equivalent in meaning to اكثر وقوع

129.

الاعور في بلاد العميان طرفة

The one-eyed person is a beauty in the country of the blind.

130.

اين تروح الشمس من القصارين

Whither can the sun retire from the bleachers?

This alludes to persons who cannot elude the pursuit of their importunate clients. The bleachers are constantly watching for the sun, that they may spread out their cloth or yarn. قصار in the dialect of Egypt, is "a bleacher."

131.*

اليد الغريبة تخرب البيوت العامرة

The foreign hand destroys the well-conditioned houses.

عامر signifies both "populous" and "in a good state of repair or cultivation."

132.

التقوا قرد يبول في مسجد قالوا له ما تخاف ربنا يمسخك
قال ان كان يعملني غزال

They met a monkey making water in a mosque, "Dost thou not fear," said they, "that the Lord may transform or metamorphose thee?" ("Indeed,") replied he, ("I should fear that punishment) if he were to change me into a Gazelle."

This refers to conceited persons. Gazelles and

monkies, according to Eastern nations, represent the
extremes of beauty and ugliness. ‏الله يمساخك‏ " May
God metamorphose thee !" is a common expression
of insult ; to which is frequently added, " may he
change thee into a dog or a hog!" ‏الله يمساخك‏
‏ماتخاف ان‏ Here is to be understood ‏كلب او خنزير‏
‏ربنا يمساخك‏.

133.

‏العادة طبع خامس‏

Custom is a fifth nature.

Arabian physiologists divide the human character
into four natural classes ; the choleric (‏دماوي‏), the
bilious (‏صفراوي‏), the melancholy (‏سوداوي‏), and the
phlegmatic (‏بلغمي‏).

134.*

‏التجار النحس ينظر ما يدخل ما ينظر ما يخرج‏

The bad neighbour sees only what enters (the house),
not what goes out (from it).

He keeps an account of what his neighbour
gains, but not of what he expends in charity ; *i.e.*,
he is blind to your good qualities and only notices
your defects.

حرف البا

135.

بعد ما ركب حرّك رِجليه

After he had mounted, he put his legs in motion (to excite the animal that he rode).

When a man is once firmly established in power, he begins to oppress and tyrannize.

136.*

بعد ما وصل الاسلام ادعي الشرف

After he had attained to Islám, he affected to be a Sheríf.

Success renders a man bold.

137.*

بدوي مقروح ولقي تمر مطروح قال اين اروح

A miserable Bedouin found a date (that had been) thrown away. " Whither shall I go," said he, ("to eat it in safety?")

Trifles become treasures to the poor. مقروح is not used by the Egyptians in its literal meaning "ulcerated," but generally to express "miserable, pitiable." They also use تمر for ثمر "a dry date."

138.

بعد ما ناكوها عشرة صاحت للغفّرة

*After they had ravished her, she called out to the
watchmen.*

On the hypocrisy of prudes. غفير in the plural
غفرة—watchmen stationed in different quarters of the
town.

139.

بيلول الريف عيار

The village saint is a clever impostor.

بيلول signifies a living sáint or half-mad man.
Egypt abounds with fellows of this description, who
are well known to be vile impostors. الريف in the
usual acceptation of the word, means the open
country and villages between Cairo and the Medi-
terranean Sea. عيار in the Egyptian dialect, a clever
active thief, an impostor.

140.*

باعت المنارة و اشترت ستارة قال دي هتيكة بحسن عبارة

*She sold the lamp and bought a curtain (to hide her
doings in the bed chamber). "That," said one,
"is a scandal under a fine appearance."*

هتيكة "scandal." Thus هتكوني "they make a
public scandal of me." The word جرسة is likewise
used in the same sense. بحسن عبارة "finely explained, giving a good external appearance."

141.

بعد ما اكل و اتكا قال داريحة عيشكم مستكي

After he had eaten and was reclining on the sofa, he said, " thy bread has a smell of mastick."

When he had fully enjoyed it he began to disparage it.   اتكا " he reclined," as people after dinner, upon sofa-cushions, when coffee is presented to them. عيش in the Egyptian dialect signifies " bread."

142.

بلدنا صغيرة و نعرف بعضنا

Our town is but small, we all know each other.

This is said when an acquaintance meditates some fraud or deception.

143.

بدال مشيك بقبقابك شيلي شراميطك من اكعابك

Instead of walking upon kabkábs, take the rags off thy heels.

Provide for the necessaries of life before you enjoy the luxuries.   بدال in the Egyptian dialect for بدل—Kabkábs are stilts or wooden slippers, four or five inches high, upon which the women walk in the baths, and the ladies of genteel rank in their houses. These latter have their kabkábs ornamented with various sorts of silver tassels, and inlaid with mother of pearl. شرموطة is used by the Egyptians for " a rag ;" also for " a vile slut."

144.

بخرا و تزاهم علي البوس

She has an offensive breath, yet presses forward to get a kiss.

On the ill-founded pretensions of people.

145.*

بيُس البديل بيدق بغيل

(That is) a bad exchange, (like giving) a pawn for a bishop.

A saying derived from the game of chess.

146.

بين حانا و بانا ضاعت الحانا

Between Háná and Báná our beards were lost.

This proverb owes its origin to a story resembling one which La Fontaine has related. Háná and Báná were the wives of an elderly man—one plucked out his grey hairs, the other his black, and so left him without any. In Egypt there are other terms, like Háná and Báná, used merely because they sound almost alike : thus "he went to *Khirt Birt*" (خرت برت), which means that he travelled upon a foolish errand ; or "he went to *Hersh Mersh*" (خرش مرش), implying that he did not succeed in his business, or else that he was placed in a state of mortification or disgrace, which might be expressed by the English saying, "he was sent to Coventry." (Other words without any literal signification used

in this manner, will occur hereafter.)   It may here
be remarked that many facetious stories long current
in Europe, are of Arabian origin.

147.

بَكِي ادم علي فراق الجنّة

(*Like*) *the lamentation of Adam on his departure or
separation from Paradise.*

This is said of unavailing grief, chiefly of lamentation for the deceased.

148.

باتت جيعانة و زوجها خبّاز

*She went to sleep hungry, (although) her husband is
a baker.*

Those nearest to plenty sometimes experience
want.   جيعانة in Egypt used for جايعة

149.

بلد ما تعرف فيها اعمل ما تشتهي فيها

*In a town where thou knowest nobody, do whatever
thou likest.*

Most people are ashamed only of those by whom
they are known.   Here is to be understood بلد
التي ما تعرف فيها احد

150.

بيت تاكل منه لا تدعي عليه بالخراب

*A house from which thou eatest, do not pray for its
destruction.*

151.

بير تشرب منه لا ترمي فيه حجر

*A well from which thou drinkest, throw not a stone
into it.*

152.

بس تحمّصها لا تحرقها

Roast them only, do not burn them.

Too violent measures cause us to lose the expected
profits. تحميص signifies the roasting of coffee-beans
in small iron pans, according to the Eastern custom ;
these pans are called محمصة The word بس is of the
Syrian or Egyptian dialect and much used ; it means
"only," "at all events," "nothing more," "this will
do," &c. ; at other times it is merely a superfluous
particle, or an expletive without meaning, annexed to
some phrase.

153.

بيع و شرا و ما في الطبلة شيء

Selling and buying, and nothing upon the board.

Equivalent to the saying, "great cry and little
wool." طبلة or طبلية is a round board on which the
pedlars who walk about the streets expose their
goods for sale.

154.

باز علي قغاز

(Like) a hawk over a scare-crow (i.e., flying about it).

To designate a person of meddling disposition,

who never remains a moment quiet. تِغَاز is a particular sort of scare-crow, made of thin pieces of wood, and used in the gardens about Cairo.

155.

ترك الذنب و لا طلب المغفرة

He left off sinning, but never asked forgiveness.

Said in allusion to those who think it sufficient if they discontinue their bad actions, but never make atonement or solicit pardon for those they have already committed.

156.

تابت القحبة ليلة قالت ولا والي يمسك القحاب

A harlot repented for one night. " Is there no police officer," she exclaimed, " to take up or lay hold of harlots ?"

Those who have been sinners themselves are often the least indulgent towards others ; and on the slightest repentance they claim the privilege of rigid virtue. قحبه (plural قحاب) the term used at Cairo to express a harlot or public woman. ولا is an exclamation. الوالي the chief police officer at Cairo. He is also entitled exclusively " El Aga."

157.

تعالوا في دي الرحمة نطاهر القليط

Come, let us circumcise the kalyt in this crowd.

A proverb ironically expressing that this is not the proper time or place for a business in question. قليط is a person suffering from certain tumours which sometimes affect even children at Cairo; and which would render the operation of circumcision extremely tedious and troublesome. Kalyt among the vulgar is a nickname frequently applied.

158.

تعالي بلا دعوة اتعدي علي دي الفروة

Come, (my dear,) without any (more) quarrelling, sit down upon this pelisse.

Said in ridicule of the means employed by a husband to coax his wife into good humour. دي for هذي In the Egyptian dialect دعوة signifies "complaint," "quarrel." To spread a pelisse that another may sit upon it is a mark of great respect and attention.

159.

تموت الحداية و عينها في الخطف

The falcon dies and his eye is (still) upon the seizure (of his prey).

The tyrant continues a tyrant to his last breath. حداية an ash-grey falcon of the smaller species,

common throughout Egypt and Syria. الخطف the
action of seizing or carrying off prey. The verb
خطف is constantly employed to express the carrying
off plunder by soldiers from peasants and shopkeepers.

160.

تطلق النار و تصيح الحريق

Thou kindlest the flame, and criest "fire."

161.

تكون نار تصبح رماد

It may be a fire; on the morrow it will be ashes.

Violent passions easily subside.

162.

تاخذ من الحافي نعله

Thou takest from the sore-footed his sandal.

Thou ruinest the man completely. حافي means
not only "bare-footed," but one who has the sole of
his foot sore from walking.

163.

تبوس الحريف تقلع اسنانه

Thou kissest thy lover, and tearest out his teeth.

On the greediness of bad women. الحريف properly means "a rival;" but in Egypt is generally
used for "a lover:" it signifies also at Cairo a partner
at the chess or backgammon board.

164.

تقرا الزبور علي اهل القبور

Thou readest the Psalms to the inhabitants of the tombs.

Thou doest what nobody else does. The Psalms are seldom read by Moslims, because they assert that the Christians have interpolated them; yet they acknowledge that David was inspired by heaven when he composed and sung them. Nobody thinks, however, of reading or reciting to the dead.

165.

تمَسَكَنوا حتي تمكنوا

They behaved like poor honest people until they were firmly established.

On the artful system of Eastern governors. تمسكنوا from the word مسكين which means not only "poor" or "humble," but also "honest;" a sense probably arising from the circumstance that in Eastern countries poor people only are honest. It sometimes implies likewise a reproach of stupidity; thus راجل مسكين "a poor, honest fool," and perhaps for a reason similar to the former; because here no one is ever blamed for cheating or deceiving others, but for allowing himself to be cheated. Few who have talents and cunning condescend to be honest; so that honesty is rather depreciated, or found only among poor fools.

166.

تبيّض بيض مدوّر و تطلب فراريج هندية

*He lays round eggs and asks for young turkeys (to
proceed from them).*

On unreasonable expectations. The turkey egg
is oval, while the pigeon egg (here meant) is nearly
round.

167.

تضارب الريح و البحر قالت المراكب دي نوبة وقعت علينا

*Wind and sea combat—" this time," said the ships,
" we shall have the worst of it."*

When two rivals contend for the government, the
subjects are most to be pitied. نوبه in the Egyptian
dialect means " for once," " this time." نوبة وقعت علينا
" for once it has fallen upon us ;" *i.e.*, the misfortune.
There is also a saying نوبة جت علينا " for once or
this time it has come upon us," (*i.e.*, the goodhap,)
or " we shall be gainers." جت used in Egypt for
جات

168.

تجري الرياح بما لا يشتهي السفّان
The wind blows as the sailors do not wish.

On untoward circumstances in general. اجري
" to run ;" it implies also any other kind of rapid
motion.

169.

تحت الكسا تيس

Under this (fine) apparel a he-goat (is hidden).

A he-goat (تيس) is, among Arabs, the emblem of a stupid clown. اسكت يا تيس " be silent, thou goat," is a phrase often heard in the bázárs.

170.

تاج المروة التواضع

The crown of a good disposition is humility.

مروة in the Egyptian dialect does not merely signify what belongs to the مر—what is *manly*, but in general " good disposition," " kindness," " zeal." It is said of a person صاحب مروة " who likes to be serviceable to others," " who is honestly zealous in his business." (ما له شي مروة) مالوش مروة " a cold egotist."

حرف الثا

171.

ثوب العارية ما يدفّي

A borrowed cloak does not keep one warm.

We best enjoy what is our own property.

172.

ثور الحرث ما يتكمم

The ox that ploughs is not to be muzzled.

This was a precept of the Jewish law. See Deute-
ronomy xxv, 4. We must necessarily trust to those
whom we employ in any business. يتكمم comes from
كمامة a muzzle made of ropes, closely tied to the
mouths of oxen, camels, and other cattle, to prevent
their grazing in the fields of strangers in passing
along the road; for there are not in Egypt any
inclosures.

173.

ثلاثة اذا اتنقوا علي بلد اخربوها

*Three (persons) if they unite against a town will
ruin it.*

The smallest number of evil-disposed persons, if
well united, can work considerable mischief.

174.

توبه ماخرق من اي مكان اشتهي يطلع يده

*His gown is full of holes; he thrusts out his hand at
whatever place he likes.*

Poverty is sometimes an advantage, as it insures
freedom of action. ثوبه for توبه

175.*

ثعبان علي قرص جلّة عايم في بركة قذر قال ما لدي البركة
المنتنة الّا دي الشاختور الاخرا و هذا المتفرّج القذر

A serpent upon a dung-cake was swimming in a dirty

pond. Some one said, (indeed,) "nothing suits this stinking pond better than this ship of dirt and this filthy spectator" (i.e., the serpent).

لهذي or الي هذي for لدي The dried cakes of cattle-dung are called جلّة—used as fuel in the East. A common term for "serpent" in Egypt is حيّة—a great serpent is called ثعبان—and this name is likewise given to the eel.

حرف الجيم

176.*

جور الترك و لا عدل العرب

The oppression of Turks, rather than the justice of Arabs.

By the term Arabs are here meant the Bedouins, who, in the Mammelouk times, most grievously oppressed the open country of Egypt. The Bedouins themselves often call their nation exclusively "Arab," a term they use more frequently than "Bedou;" and all other Arabians, who are not of Arab tribes, they distinguish by the appellation of Hadhary or Fellah, which with them are terms of reproach or contempt.

177.*

جور القط و لا عدل الفار

*The tyranny of the cat, rather (or is better) than the
justice of the mouse.*

The mouse bears a much worse character in the
East than in the West; "wily, insidious, rapacious,"
are the gentlest epithets applied to her. Mice are
certainly a great nuisance in Egypt, where the open
country (as well as every town) abounds with them
to such a degree, that I have known instances of
families being actually driven from their homes by
the numbers and rapaciousness of the mice and rats,
that spared neither victuals nor furniture. جور signifies "unjust, violent, oppressive behaviour."

178.

جيت ادعي عليه رايت الحيط مايل عليه

*I came to utter an imprecation against him, and
found the wall inclining over him.*

It is unnecessary to revile a person who is already
crushed by universal opprobrium. مايل عليه "inclining over him," "ready to fall upon him."

179.

جواب النحس علي طرف لسانه

The fool has his answer on the edge of his tongue.

The fool answers without reflection, whatever
comes first into his mind. نحس here means "a fool."

not merely "vile or bad." The following verse is
quoted on the same subject :

لسان العاقل في قلبِهِ   و قلب الاحتى في فمه

The tongue of the wise is in his heart,
The heart of the fool is in his mouth.

180.

جواب الاحتى السكات عنه

Silence is the (best) answer to the stupid.

السكات عنه means likewise "to leave him alone."
اسكت عنه "leave him alone" is a common expression,
signifying "neither speak to him nor meddle with
him."

181.

جا عند الزنادقة يكفر

He came to the impious to blaspheme.

He did what was superfluous, because all his
companions did the same. With a similar meaning
the Arabs say تحصيل حاصل "a (second) receipt for
what has already been settled," or equally superfluous actions.

182.

جا التخروف يعلّم ابوه الرعي

The lamb came to teach its father how to feed.

183.

جاءوا لينعلوا خيل الباشا فمدّت التخنفسة رجلها

They came to shoe the horses of the Pâshá; the beetle
then stretched out its leg (to be shod).

On ridiculous pretensions.

184.

جمل موضع جمل يبرك

The camel crouches down on the place of another camel.

This is said when one great dignitary dies and another immediately takes his place. In travelling, the places where the camels repose on the evening station are distinguished from the surrounding country, and caravans usually halt at the same spots.

185.*

جبّ ما يمتلي من الندا

A well is not to be filled with dew.

This is said when trifling presents are offered to a powerful person who is known to be greedy.

186.

جيت الاقرع يونسني كشفَ راسه و خوّفني

I came to the scabby-headed (person) to be amused in his company; he uncovered his head and frightened me.

Friendship ceases when a person's real character is known.

187.

جا واحد يعدّ امواج البحر غلط قال التجيات اكثر من الرايحات

One came to count the waves of the sea; he erred (in the reckoning). " There are (at all events) more coming than going," he said.

On paltry expedients to conceal ignorance or

negligence. The expression اللجيات اكثر من الرايحات
is likewise often used to console a person for some
disappointment, and then it means "one opportunity
is lost, but another will present itself." جيات in the
Egyptian dialect for جايات

188.

جوا يحلبوا التيس ضرط

They came to milk the goat; he br—ke w—nd.

The stupid clown disappoints those who require
his services. جوا used in Egypt for جاءوا

189.

جهد المقل دموعه

The efforts of the poor are his tears.

The poor can only weep for the misfortunes of
others, but are not able to alleviate them; this is a
frequent apology for withholding assistance.

190.

جارك معلمك

Thy neighbour is thy teacher.

We learn from our companions.

191.

جوع القملة في راس الاقرع

*(Like) the hunger of the louse upon the head of the
scabby.*

Is said when a person in affluence pleads poverty.

192.*

جا الهم عند الهم يحدث

Grief came to converse with grief.

The afflicted cannot console the afflicted.

193.*

جنازة غريب لا وراه و لا قدامه

(Like) the burial of a stranger, no one goes before and
no one behind him.

This is said of a person who retires from office
without the regret of any one. لا وراه is to be understood as لا وراه احد

194.*

جندي ما قبل شيع طرطوره

The (intercession of the) soldier was not accepted, he
(then) sent the soldier's cap (to intercede for him).

If the patronage of the master cannot serve, that
of the servant can be of little avail. In Egypt جندي
implies a horse soldier, in opposition to a foot soldier
or عسكري—The Egyptians use شيع as the common
term for "to send." طرطور is the high woollen or fur
cap worn by the horsemen, called *dely* or *delaty.*

195.

جنة ترعاها الخنازير

A paradise in which hogs feed.

Said of a beautiful woman whose husband is ugly.

196.

جهلٌ يعولني خيرٌ من عقل اعوله

*Ignorance that supports me is better than wisdom
which I must support.*

Rather take from the fool, than give to the wise.

197.

جهلك اشد من كفرك

Thou art more ignorant even than thou art impious.

Verbatim : "thy ignorance is stronger than thy
impiety." The word كافر is a very common term of
insult among the Moslim Egyptians themselves, and
means, when applied by one of them to another,
"impious."

198.

الجمل في شي و الجمّال في شي

*The camel has his projects, and the camel driver has
his projects.*

The interests of the governor and the governed
are never alike. في شي is here to be understood as
نيته في شي.

199.*

اجلس حيث يوخذ بيدك و تبذل لا حيث يوخذ
برجلك و تَجَرِّ

Sit down when thou art taken by the hand and when

*thou receivest presents ; and not when they lay
hold of thy leg and drag thee (away).*

Visit only where thou art welcome. With respect
to the expression يوخذ بيدك some remarks shall be
offered hereafter.

حرف الحاء

200.

حماتك مناقرة طلّق بنتها

*Is thy mother-in-law quarrelsome ? Divorce her
daughter.*

Cut up the evil by the root. The mother and
daughter will leave thy house together.

201.

حبيبي مليح و يتعمّم بنخ

*(In truth) my lover is a fine fellow, and he wears a
straw turban.*

Said in derision of a ridiculous spark. يتعمّم " to
tie," and " to wear a turban." بنخ are the mats made
of dry reeds in which is packed the charcoal sent to
Cairo from the country about Thebes.

202.

حزينة ما لها بقر فتلت شِعرتها فرقلة

Afflicted, because she has no cows; she twisted her hair into a whip.

Said of one who consoles himself for the want of enjoyments by mere phantasms. فِرقلة is a whip made of date-leaves, with which the peasants drive their oxen in ploughing or drawing at the water-mills; it is likewise called رخو—The word شِعرة must not be confounded with شعر or "hair," although I have so translated it; this latter means the "hair of the head;" but شعرة those hairs which in the East it is usual to shave off or remove by a depilatory, although the slovenly peasant-women often allow them to grow for months.

203.*

حزينة ما لها بيت اشترت مكنسة و زيت

Afflicted at having no house, she bought a broomstick and some oil.

Of the same signification as the proverb immediately preceding.

204.

حزينة ما لها عينين اشترت مراية بدرهمين

Aggrieved because she had no eyes, she purchased a looking-glass for two derhems.

Of the same import. مراة for مراية

205.

حسبنا؛ حساب [الحية و العقرب و ام اربعة و اربعين ما
كانت لنا في حساب

*In our account we reckoned the serpent and the
scorpion; but the "erba wa erbayn" was not in
our reckoning.*

We have not taken proper precautions against
the most dangerous enemy. The *"erba wa erbayn"*
is a small spider-like insect, which is said to have
forty-four feet, whence it derives its name. It is
reputed extremely venomous. I never happened to
see one.

206.

حلبوا قردة كشّت قالوا اللبن اللي يجي من دي
الوجه حرام

*They milked a monkey; she drew back in a surly
manner. "The milk," said they, "which comes
from (one with) that face is (surely) bad
stuff."*

The wretch who with affectation and grimace
refuses to assist others by a service that would reflect
honour on himself, will never do any good. يكشّ in
the Egyptian dialect means "to draw back sulkily,"
or like a prude or coquette, if any one approach too
near. حرام not only signifies "unlawful" or "forbidden," but in common speech, "worthless."

207.

حاقة بلا جاه صفع حاضر

Anger without power (is) a blow ready.

If a person become angry with another to whom
he is inferior in strength, he may expect to receive a
blow. حاقة in the Egyptian dialect signifies "anger,"
as well as "stupidity." It is said, تحمقت منه " I
became angry with him." جاه is "official power,
influence, importance, patronage derived from rank
or wealth." صفع equivalent to تفا "a blow on the
neck."

208.

حلّني من عامود لعامود لعل ياتي فرج

*Loose me from pillar to pillar; perchance it may
cause liberation.*

Loose my chains from one pillar, and fasten them
to another, said a prisoner, perhaps in so doing I may
effect my release. This signifies, that the unfortunate
grasp at the most trifling circumstance in hopes of
relief. Among other meanings فرَج implies deliverance, relief, return of good luck, an opening to happier
circumstances. In this sense God is styled فراج—
and when Arabs pray for deliverance from misfortunes they always address him by this name, and say
يا فراج—The expression فيه فرج is often used in like
manner to console a person, and then means "hope
the best!"

209.

حجر في دكان زجاج

A storm in the shop of a glass-dealer.

Signifying that a thing is quite out of place. زجّاج a dealer in glass-ware.

210.

حطّه في قفّة الملوخية طلع في قفّة البادنجان

*He put him into the basket of Meloukhye; he came
out of the basket of Bádenján.*

Said of one who is continually running about and seen almost at the same time in different parts of the town, always in great haste. The *Meloukhye* is corchorus olitorius, a favourite vegetable among the Egyptians. *Bádenján*, the egg-plant, is likewise much esteemed by them.

211.

حزينة ما لها دار عملت تقبتها زريبة

*Afflicted because she had no house, she made a livery
stable of the hole (in which she lived).*

On the ridiculous attempts of poor people to imitate the great, or to appear rich. تقبة for نقبة means a "hole," more particularly foramen ani. In derision this term is applied to a small dirty place where poor persons live. زريبة a public stable wherein cows are kept in the town at that season when the open country is inundated. Similar stables are found in every quarter of the town, and the cows kept therein furnish Cairo with milk during the inundation.

212.

حكّ رغيف برغيف لا بد من لبابه

Rub a loaf against a loaf, no doubt of its crumbs
(coming forth).

Set two men of equal powers against each other,
their true character will appear from that experiment.

213.

حول باب اصطبلك

Remove the gate of thy stable to another side.

This is generally said on averting the danger of
the evil eye. If a house is reputed of evil omen
(شوم), the owner usually walls up the gate, and
opens one at another side, by which he hopes to
avert the baneful consequences of the evil eye of
his enemies. اصطبل (or اسطبل) is the origin of
"stabulum," a stable.

214.

حلو اللسان بعيد الاحسان

Sweet of tongue (but) of far distant beneficence.

Said of a hypocrite.

215.

حسبنا في البيداء رجال

We thought that there were men in the desert.

Said of persons whose cowardice has disappointed
our expectations. حسب is often employed in the
sense of "thinking;" thus حسبت انك تحبني "I
thought thou lovedst me."

216.

حكم القوي علي الضعيف

(*Like*) *the government of the strong over the weak.*

Applied to unjust oppressions in private life.

217.

حرّة صبرت بيتها عمرت

*A virtuous woman had patience (with her husband),
her house flourished (or continued well peopled).*

البيت عمرت means here "to be peopled," or to
continue inhabited by all its inmates; in opposition to
بيتها خربت words which would have been used if her
husband had divorced her and she had left the house:
here is to be understood حرّة ان صبرت

218.

حديثكم طيّب و بيتنا بعيد

Your talking is fine, but our house is far distant.

In spite of all your fine reasoning I am far from
complying with your desire. حديث is often used
in Egypt synonymously with كلام as the verb يتحدث
is used instead of يتكلم

219.*

حدبا عرجا و يدها اليمين فلجا

Crook-backed, limping, her right hand trembling.

Denoting a woman afflicted with every kind of
misery. فالج in the Egyptian dialect, means one
who labours under a tremor produced by extreme

debility. Instead of يمين it ought to be يمنة—because
يد is feminine; but the Egyptians very often con-
found the genders. It may, however, be possibly
understood here as يدها من جانب اليمين

220.

حبّك الحبّ و بغضك الرب

*May the ulcer (of the Franks) love thee, and the Lord
hate thee.*

Addressed to a hypocritical enemy who assures
us of his friendship, and says, "I love thee," or
انا احبّك The word الحبّ is here put for الحب
الفرنجي "the ulcer of the Frank," or "the French
disease."

221.

حاسدتها تعتر في شعرتها

May her envier stumble over her hair.

An imprecation against the enemy or jealous
rival of a woman. تعتر in the Egyptian dialect for
تعثر See above, No. 202, for a remark on شعرة —It
means, "may he be unlucky whenever he approaches
her."

222.

حبّة تتقل الميزان

A single grain makes the balance heavier.

Where two parties of equal power contend, a
very slight accession of strength will decide the
question in favour of one. تثقل for تتقل

223.

حبلة و مرضعة و قدامها اربعة

She is with child, and nurses a child, and has four (children) before her.

On affluence of riches.

224.

حساب القوآر علي الدوآر

The (broken) pots are put to the account of the retailer.

Great people make the poor pay for the mishaps that befall them. قوآر in the Egyptian dialect "pots and jars of earth." It is to be understood here القوار المكسرين The name of الدوآر is given to these who carry the earthenware upon their heads about the streets, on account of the manufacturers. If any of them should break, those who carry them are responsible to their principals.

225.

حلم القطط كله فيرأن

The dream of the cat is all about the mice.

226.

حلفا و ٚيحاشر النار

(Like) dry reeds and (still) keeps company with the fire.

Most likely to suffer from the calamity yet imprudently exposing himself to it. حلفا is the *arundo epigeios,* that grows particularly in Upper Egypt in districts which are not regularly inundated : the poor people use it as fuel. يعاشر is the Egyptian pronunciation of يعاشر The lower classes frequently pronounce the ع like ح Thus they say عشر اربحت for عشر اربعة—also معصرة for محصرة—and له حت for له بعت—likewise رحت for وجعت—حت for جعت—but the same people pronounce the ع strongly in other words when it is placed at the beginning or end of them

227.*

حبيبك من تحبه و لو كان قرد

Thy beloved is the object that thou lovest, were it even
a monkey.

Love is blind.

حرف الخاء

228.

خير الزاد ما حصل في الفواد

The best food is that which fills the belly.

Such is the true though not the literal meaning. فواد is taken here for the whole of the intestines. حصل "to reach, to arrive at, to hit, to fulfil one's purpose, to satiate."

229.

خطبوها تمنَّعت تركوها تطلَّعت

They wooed her, and she resisted; they left her, and she then fell in love.

On the whims of those who capriciously oppose the wishes of others. تطلَّع among several significations, means, in the Egyptian dialect, the same as تتشوق "to fall in love," because it is understood تطلَّعت علي العاشق

230.

خبّاز و محتسب

Baker and (at the same time) Mohteseb.

His interest will cause him to lose sight of his duty. Mohteseb is the public officer who superintends the legal price and weight of the provisions sold in the bázár.

231.*

خذي بختك من حجر اختك

Take thy luck from the lap of thy sister.

A poor woman complained that she had not any children, her sister had half-a-dozen little ones in her lap, and did not know how to supply them with food. The person is therefore advised to take warning from her and not to form rash wishes.

232.

خرا العمل و لا زعفران البطاله

The dirt of labour rather than the saffron of indolence.

Rather to be busy were it even in dirty work or labour of little profit, than to be indolent though in possession of luxuries.

233.

خلال ما يحب خلال

A vinegar seller does not like (another) vinegar seller.

On the " jalousie de métier." At Cairo the name of الخلال is given to the sellers of pickles ; cucumbers, turnips, onions, badenjáns (egg-plants) preserved in date vinegar are favourites with the Egyptians.

234.

خذ العلم و التخبر من خراطيم البقر

Acquire learning and information (even if they come)
from the mouths of cows.

Never object to any source from which you may derive useful knowledge. خرطوم is the snout of a hog, and generally applied to any ugly mouth.

235.

خذ من الغريم و لو حجر

Take from the (bad) debtor were it but a stone.

Do not refuse from a bad debtor whatsoever he

may pay on account. In receiving a small part of a considerable debt, it is often said,

شعرة من الخنزير احسن من ذقنه

A single bristle of the hog is better than all his (the bad debtor's) beard.

236.

خنفسة علي مكنسة داخلة المستراح قال انظر الحامل المحمول
و دار الوكالة

A beetle upon a broomstick was entering the privy; "look," said one, "at the carrier, the carried, and the hotel!"

The دار الوكالة are public khans at Cairo, where strangers halt and merchandise is deposited. The abridged saying, "look at the carrier and the carried," is often quoted on seeing a mean looking man riding upon a wretched Rosinante.

237.

خردة بلا عدة

Toys without instruments.

خردة small ware and other toys sold usually in the same shop. عدة implements used in the different crafts. The saying implies, "fuss about trifles," "much ado about nothing." A man keeps toys in his shop, but not any useful or necessary implements.

238.

خلّاها علي الارض السودا

He left her upon the black ground.

He ruined her completely. In taking away her
mat, the poorest article of household furniture, he left
her to sit upon the bare floor.

239.

خيار الناس مَن كسبوا عليه

*Those are (esteemed) the best people through whom
one gains.*

The expression مَن كسبوا عليه stands for علي يد مَن
كسبوا علي يد الذين or "upon whose hand they gained,"
i.e., through whose interference or medium.

240.

خيار البِّر عاجله

The best generosity is that which is quick.

241.

خير ما تعمل شر ما تلقي

Do no good—thou shalt not find evil.

On ingratitude.

242

خلوا العزل المخبّل لدي القلب المدبل

*Leave the entangled yarn to be untwisted by the
effeminate or pusillanimous.*

المخبّل interwoven, intricate, disordered ; this
sense is likewise expressed by مُلَخبَط The word المدبل

in the Egyptian dialect for ذابل signifies "effeminate," "weak-hearted," "unable to make exertion."
لدي for لهذي This saying means that the business
must be suited to the capacity or character of a man,
and the puny or weak-hearted must be employed
in women's work.

243.*

خاوي البطن و يمضغ لبان

Of empty stomach, yet he chews incense.

A hungry beggar, yet affecting the manners of
great people. It is a common practice in Egypt
among the higher classes to chew incense in order
to sweeten the breath; or, as it is said, to facilitate
digestion.

244.

خذ من عقله و حطه في المرجونة

*Take his understanding and put it into the basket (at
thy back).*

Said in derision of a person's understanding.
مرجونة is a small basket which the poor Nubians,
who come to try their fortunes at Cairo, sling upon
their back, and carry in it their food and miserable
luggage.

245.

خير المال ما وجهته وجهه

*Those are the best riches which are spent in their
proper place.*

Literally, "which are directed towards the proper
side."

246.

خير الناس من فرح للناس بالخير

He is the chosen of the people who rejoices in the
welfare of others.

247.

الخرق يالرفق يلحم

With gentleness the fracture is repaired.

With politeness and softness a reconciliation can
be effected in quarrels. This refers to the common
saying, خرق خرق في الصحبة "a hole has been bored
in the friendship," or "friends have been disunited."

248.

الخضوع عند الحاجات رجولية

To be humble when we want (the help of others) is
manliness.

This maxim is deeply impressed on the minds of
people in the East. الحاجات "affairs," "business,"
"wants," "demands from others," &c.

249.

اخرج الطمع من قلبك يحل القيد من رجلك

Expel avidity from thy heart; the fetters will be
loosened from thy foot.

Be contented, and thou wilt be free.

250.

خلّوه بهمّه اخذ واحدة قدر أمه

*Leave him alone with his grief—he has taken one as
old as his mother.*

Of one who deserves his misfortunes. The man
had married an old woman, and might therefore have
expected from the first not to be very happy with her.
اخذ is often used for زوج "he married." قدر "similar
to anything in quantity or quality;" often employed
in the same sense as مثل

251.

خذها من سكران و لا تاخذها من صاحي

*Take (the wine) from the drunkard and do not take it
from the sober.*

The sober will more probably betray thee in this
instance than the drunkard. The ها of خذها refers
to خمرة or "wine." صاحي "one who is awake," "in
possession of his senses," "sober."

252.

خذ الكتاب من عنوانه

*Take the book by its title; or, take the letter by its
address.*

The first view teaches us to judge of a person's
character, and whether he be a fit object for a nearer
acquaintance. Such is generally thought in the
East, where a Lavaterian system of physiognomy
prevails. Every governor of a province is a phy-

siognomist, and fancies that he can ascertain in the looks or mien of those brought before him which is the guilty party. A prepossessing face has more influence in the East than in Europe ; but the rules of physiognomy are never strictly analysed, and it is chiefly from the expression of the eyes and the state of the eyebrows and nose that an opinion is formed.

253.

خبزه مخبوز و ماءه في الكوز

His bread is kneaded and his water is in the jug.

كوز is a small earthen or tin jug, by which water is taken out of the large jars that stand in the vestibule of each house in Egypt.

254.

خذ بلاش قال ما يسع التليس

Take it for nothing. (" No,") he said, " my sack is not large enough (to contain it)."

On the great luck of some to whom more is offered than they can accept. تليس is a sack of black or white and black striped goat hair, in which the peasants carry their corn to market. بلاش for بلاشي is the common expression in Egypt for " gratis."

255.

خذ طينة و اضربها في الحيط ان ما لزقت اثرت

Take a piece of mud, strike it against the wall, if it do not stick it will leave a mark.

On the effects of slander.

256.

خيال خرا و يرمح في النخل

A bad rider—yet he gallops about among the date-trees.

This is said of the ignorant who affect to display learning. خرا "dirt," is often used to express a "thing as bad as dirt," "useless," "miserable." يرمح "to set off the horse in full gallop," "to ride at full speed." To gallop among date-trees is of course difficult on account of the numerous turnings.

257.

خذ اللص قبل ان ياخذك

Take the thief before he take thee.

258.

خذ بيدي اليوم اخذ برجلك غدا

Take me by the hand to-day, I will take thee by the foot to-morrow.

Be kind to me now, I will hereafter return the favour two-fold. خذ بيدي is equivalent to خذ يدي "take my hand," or "assist me." The beggars at Cairo constantly say الله ياخذ بيد الكريم "God assists the charitable and generous." الله ياخذ بيدك "May God assist thee." The expression "I will take thee by the foot," means that on a future occasion I will assist thee more powerfully than thou assistest me at present.

259.

خاطر من استغني برايه

*He exposes himself (to danger) who regards his own
counsel or opinion as sufficient.*

استغني is here in the same sense as اكتفي   But
this is not the usual signification of the word in
Egypt, where it commonly means " not to be in want
of."   Thus a very frequent expression is استغنيت عنه
" I do not want it," " I can dispense with it."

260.

خذ القليل من اللئيم و ذمه

*Take the merest trifle from the vile and abuse him (at
the same time).*

The miser deserves no better treatment. اللئيم
is here put for البخيل " the miser." الذم properly
signifies " to reproach a person with his bad qualities,"
or ذكر المعايب

حرف الدال

261.

دار الظالم خراب و لو بعد حين

*The house of the unjust oppressor is (or must be) des-
troyed, though it should happen in distant times.*

262.

ديار مصر خيرها لغريبها

The riches of Egypt are for the foreigners therein.

Since the time of the Pharaohs Egypt has never been governed by national rulers, but constantly by foreigners. دار مصر is said in the same sense as دار النوبة or دار فور

263.

دخل شي في اضراسه ما بَقِي يتخرج

Something has entered into his back teeth that will never come out again.

This is applied to a person who cannot rid himself of a disagreeable companion or confidant. The word بَقِي pronounced "*baka,*" is constantly employed as an adverb, sometimes quite superfluously and without any meaning; at other times it signifies "now," "again," "then," "never."

264.

دموع الفواجر حواضر

The tears of the adultress are ever ready.

265.

دار و بوّابه ما يعتر الغار فيها بلبابه

A house with its gate—and the monk cannot find a crumb of bread in it.

On the stinginess of a person in easy circumstances. "A house with its gate," implies that it is a well-conditioned dwelling. يعثر for يعثر "to stumble," "to make a false step," and therefore "to sin;" likewise "to find," or "light upon." بوابة is often used synonymously with باب—at other times it means a "by-gate." The gates which inclose the interior quarters of the town are called بوابة

266.

دبّ لا يتحلب و لا يتجنب و لا يركب

(Like) a bear that is neither to be milked, nor to be led in parade, nor to be ridden.

Said of a useless clown. دبّ often pronounced دبّ is a "bear." Turks from Anadolia sometimes exhibit bears in shows at Cairo. A large party of those Turks came in 1814 from Romelia to Cairo with half-a-dozen bears. The people then said, that in Mohammed Aly's country (he is a native of the sea coast of Romelia,) every man was a dancing master to a bear, and that the pasha had sent for them to remind him of his youthful pursuits. On the spreading of this report the bears and their masters were immediately banished from the country. يتجنب comes from جنيب a horse led in parade before a great man in public processions.

267.

دسوتهم عالية و بطونهم خاليت

Their boilers are high; their stomachs are empty.

Costly furniture in a house, but no provisions nor

money. دسوت is the plural of دست "a boiler," or
"large pan."

268.

دَق علي الباب قال من دا قال كس بلاش قال ادخل
و لو انك سمّ الموت

There was a knock at the door. "Who is there?"
"A wench for nothing." "Enter," he said, "even
if thou wert the poison of death."

What is given gratis is always acceptable; and
according to that rule no one in the East, from the
lowest to the highest, refuses a present. On this
subject the following proverb also is cited:

اللي بلاش كترّ منه اللي بغلوس حوّد عنه

What is for nothing, get still more of it; what is for
money, avoid it.

حوّد عنه "take another road that you may not
meet it." من دا for من هذا is the common interro-
gation at Cairo for "who is there?" In Syria they
say من دا and likewise منه هذا instead of من هو هذا

كس is not properly "a wench;" its true meaning
may be found in the dictionaries. It is a term heard
much more frequently in public than Europeans
would suppose, who generally entertain very false
notions concerning the modesty and decency of the
Easterns, with respect at least to language.

269.

دود الخلّ منه

The worms of the vinegar are of the vinegar itself.

This is said when something disagreeable happens
in a family caused by one of its ill-natured members.

270*.

دع ما راب و كل ما طاب

*Leave (or do not think on) what is spoiled, but eat the
good things (that are before thee).*

راب in the Egyptian dialect is the same as تلف
"to be spoiled," and is principally said of food.
ما طاب "what fell to thy lot of good things." The
sense of this proverb is expressed in the following
ancient verses :

خذ من زمانك ما صفا ودع الذي فيه الكدر
فالعمر اقصر من معاتبة الزمان علي الغَيَر

271.

دار الحُقّ علي غطاه لَّا لتقاه

*The box went in search of its lid until it met
with it.*

On a person's eagerly watching an opportunity
and at last finding it. الحُقّ is a small box made
of ivory or bone wherein perfumes, balm, civet,
musk, &c., are sold. لَّا in the Egyptian dialect
often implies, as here, the same as حتي and then
means "until."

272.

الدّراهم مراهم

Money is sweet balm.

It heals all wounds.   Such is the general opinion
in the East.

273.

الذّابة تساوي مقرعة

The animal is worth (no more than) a whip.

As much as to say " it is worth nothing."   مقرعة
is a scourge or whip made of date-branches cut into
thin slips, still holding together like a harlequin's
wand : children play with it.   تساوي   " it is equal,"
" it is like," and more usually " it is worth."   In
Egypt it is pronounced as if written يسوا—thus they
say,   ايش يسوا   " what is it worth ?"   " what is the
price of it ?"

274.

دوا الدهر الصبر عليه

The remedy against (bad) times is to have patience
with them.

In their nervous language the ancient Arabs said,

واكلت دهرك اربعين و اربعاً فاصبر لاكلته و عضة نابه

Thou hast eaten (or enjoyed) thy age for forty-four

years; wait then when it preys upon thee with its back teeth.

الدهر is sometimes limited to the space of forty-four years, or the computed age of man.

275.

دنياک ما انت فيه

(That is) thy world wherein thou findest thyself.

Enjoy the present moment. ما انت فيه stands for الشي ما انت فيه or الحال ما انت فيه The فيه cannot relate to دنيا which is of the feminine gender.

حرف الذال

276.*

ذكروا مصر للقاهرة قامت باب اللوق بحشايشها

They mentioned Misr to Kahera; on which Báb el Look rose with its weeds.

In ridicule of those who push themselves forwards to attract notice while nobody pays them attention. They mentioned *Misr* (or *Fostát,* the first-built Moslim city, southward of the present Cairo,) to *Kahera,* the town erected by the Fatemites, on the north of *Fostát. Báb el Look* is a small and at present half-ruined quarter formerly belonging to to Fostát, but now included within the environs of Southern Cairo ; it is in many places quite deserted and abounds with grass and weeds ; it had, therefore, but slight pretensions for standing up when Misr (or Fostát) was mentioned, of which it formed one of the worst quarters or rather suburbs.

277.

ذكروا النبي بكوا قال اسمعوا ايش قال

They mentioned the Prophet ; the people wept. "Hear," cried one, "what he said" (rather than weep).

278.

ذا سنبوسك ما احناش حشوه

That is a patty, (they said,) but we are not (fit to be) its stuffing.

A fine affair ; but not one in which we can participate. سنبوسك is a flat meat patty sold in the bázár. احنا according to the Egyptian pronunciation for نحن . حشو "the *hashed* meat and spices with which patties and other dishes are stuffed." The ش of احناش is the common appendage to nouns and verbs in the Egyptian dialect.

279.

ذاك اللون اقلعه من اسنانك

Pull this dish out of thy teeth.

This is not made for you. لون in the Egyptian dialect "a dish of cooked victuals."

280.

ذا زرب ما يسدّ ريح

That is a lattice-work that does not keep off wind.

On half-measures. زرب is a lattice-work used as sheds in gardens, or upon balconies, which are usually covered with vines or creeping plants. It is made of the بوص or dry canes of the durra. ذا for هذا. يسدّ "to keep off, to stop or hinder."

281.

ذا شغل المعلّم لابنّه

That is (like) the master's work for his son.

In praise of nice and well-executed work.

282.

ذي لزقة بيطارية

That is a plaster like (the plaster) of a horse doctor.

Said of a coarse remedy applied to some evil. بيطار "the horse-smith," who, at Cairo, is likewise veterinary surgeon.

283.

ذي شي ارخص من الصكّ

That is a thing cheaper than a blow.

It is of a very low price. صكّ or سكّ "a blow on the neck."

284.

ذا جوع يفتت الزَرَد

That is a hunger that breaks a cuirass.

Said of boundless avidity or greediness. يفتت in the Egyptian dialect is often used for يكسِّر " to break." زرد " a coat of mail," " a cuirass."

285.*

ذنب الكلب عمره ما يستقيم

A dog's tail never stands straight.

Said of incorrigible habits. عمره " during his whole life," is often used for ابد " never," without any reference to life-time.

286.*

ذبابة ما هي شي و تغلّت الروح

A fly is nothing; yet it creates loathsomeness.

The most insignificant person may prove disagreeable. تَغَلَّتَ in the Egyptian dialect " to excite disgust," "to become loathsome." تغلت منه " he has disgusted me." Of the same sense is the term تقرف

287.

ذل العزل يضحك من تيه الولاية

The removal from office which is despised, laughs at the pride of government.

When we have departed from our station we

begin to see what was ridiculous in it. ذُلّ the "dis-
dained, despised, mean, miserable." This is here
personified together with العزل which is the removal
from office, rank, or power. تيه "puffed up pride."

288.

ذر مُشكل القول و ان كان حقا

Leave off ambiguous talking, should it even be true.

289.*

ذل مَن لا سفيه له

Debased is he who has no impudent defender.

سفيه "insolent, impudent." So are called in
Egypt those persons whom their masters, patrons, or
friends employ in fighting their quarrels or in disputing for them with their insolent behaviour and
impudent language: people of this kind are easily
found at Cairo. The following verse expresses the
same sense:

و مَن يحلم و ليس له سفيه يلاقي المعضلات من الرجال

290.

ذكرني فمك حمار اهلي

Thy mouth put me in mind of the jackass at home (or
of my family).

On a person appearing well at first, but proving
a worthless object on nearer view. A young man
followed a woman in the street thinking her pretty;

when she led him to a remote corner and lifted up
her veil, he discovered her ugliness, and exclaimed
in those words.

291.

ذهبت الناس و بقي النسناس

The people went away; the baboons remained.

نسناس is a species of the monkey tribe, I believe
a baboon. بقي in the Egyptian dialect is seldom
conjugated; it ought here to be بقيت

حرف الرآ

292.

راحت السكرة و جات الفكرت

Drunkenness departed and reflection came.

293.

رزق الكلاب علي المجانين

Dogs are left to be provided for by fools.

The extravagant fool throws away his money upon
those who little deserve it. رزق here means "the
lot," or "whatever is assigned by destiny." In this
sense it is often employed, and we find it so in the

Korán. To this sentence we might here suppose prefixed جَعَل الله In Syria the term رزق is often used to express " merchandise," which in Egypt is called بضاعة

294.

رزقت القردة وردة

A rose fell to the lot of a monkey.

Said of persons little deserving their good luck.

295.

رأيتك حاج و الناس راجعين

I saw thee go on the pilgrimage at the same time that the people returned from it.

On tardiness.

296.

راح يتوضّي غرق

He went to make his ablutions in a pond and was drowned.

He expected some advantage, but instead of it met with total ruin.

297.

رحم الله امه كانت اقود من ابوه

God bless his mother ; she was more profligate than his father.

Reviling language. اقود from قواد (see Dictionary). The meaning of رحم الله is literally " God have mercy ;" but in vulgar use the phrase corresponds rather with the English " God bless him !"

298.

رزق غدا لغدا

The provision for to-morrow belongs to the morrow.

Do not trouble thyself about futurity.

299.

ردّوا لنا مقطفنا ما نريد عنب

Give us back our basket, we do not wish for any grapes (therein).

Pay what thou owest us only, we want no profit from it. مقطف a basket made of date-leaves, in which the servants bring fruits and vegetables from the market.

300.

رمية من غير رامي

A throw without a thrower.

This is said in excuse of a loose word inadvertently dropped and giving offence to another person.

301.

راح مني بشحم كلاه

He went away from me together with the fat of the kidneys.

Used to express that the person left me and took away even the smallest trifle of what was due to

him; so that he has no further demands on me.
When a sheep is killed by a private person some of
the bystanders often take away the kidneys, or at
least the fat that incloses them, as due to the public
from him who slaughters the sheep.　كلاه is the
Egyptian plural of كلية "kidney."

302.

روح احمض ما عندك اطبخه

Go, (and) the most sour thou hast, cook it.

An answer to one who excuses himself on pre-
tence of the bad state of his larder for not being
able to entertain a guest. In the vulgar Egyptian
dialect روح is the imperative instead of رح

303.

رحم الله من زار و خفّف

God bless him who pays visits, and short visits.

The visits in the East, and chiefly those paid by
women to each other, sometimes last a whole day;
and even the visits of men are usually prolonged to
a most unreasonable length.　خفّف "to lighten,"
" cause to be less heavy," and here "to shorten."

304.

راح يخطب اتزوج

*He went to woo (her for a friend) and married her
himself.*

On an agent taking possession of the profits

that he was employed to earn for his principal.
اتزوّج in the Egyptian dialect for تزوّج

305.*

رحم الله امرأ عرف قدره و كفي الناس شره .

*Blessed be the man who knows his power and abstains
from doing evil to others.*

306.

راسه في القبلي و استه في الخرابة

*His head turned towards the Kebly, his hinder parts
among ruins.*

On the hypocrisy of devotees, who seem attentive
to their religious duties while they are occupied in
base worldly affairs.

307.*

راس في السما و است في الماء

The head in the heavens, the hinder parts in water.

On pride assumed by low people.

308.

ركوب الخنتافس و لا المشي علي الطنافس

*Riding (though) upon a beetle, rather than walking
upon carpets.*

Persons of high rank in Egypt hold walking in
great horror ; and after they have passed the years

of childhood, are rarely seen on foot beyond the
thresholds of their own houses. طنافس is the plural
of طنفسة "a carpet :" it is more usually called ساجادة
in Egypt.

309.

رَضِيَ الخَصمان و ابَي القاضي

*The two parties (who had been) contending agreed (to
it), but the kadhy refused his consent.*

Said when the arbitrator, from an interested
motive, endeavours to prolong the quarrel.

310.

ريح في قفص

(Like) wind in a cage.

Said of frivolous nonsensical actions and of
measures that cannot have any effect. قفص a cage
made of loosely interwoven palm-leaves.

311.*

رّبَ صَبابة غَرست من لحظة

*Sometimes love has been implanted by one glance
alone.*

312.*

رّبَ حرب شبّت من لفظة

*(The fire of) more than one war has been enkindled
by a single word.*

313.

ربَّما شَرَقَ شارب الما قبل رِيّه

Perhaps the drinker of water is nearly choked by it,
and spits it out before his thirst be quenched.

We must sometimes abandon a business which
seemed profitable at first, but proves ruinous before
the conclusion of it. شَرَقَ in the Egyptian dialect,
signifies the gurgling noise made in the throat by
spitting out water that nearly chokes one In the
same dialect ربَّما signifies "perhaps," or "it may
sometimes happen;" the more common meaning is
"perhaps."

حرف الزين

314.

زوج الصّرتين قفا بين دِرتين

The husband of two parrots (is like) a neck between
two sticks (that strike it).

On the misfortunes of a man married to two
quarrelsome and garrulous women.

315.

زقاق ضيّق و الحمار رفّاص

A narrow lane, and the ass (upon which one rides)
is kicking.

Said of those who cause additional difficulties in

an intricate business, instead of carrying us through
it. يرفص is the common term expressing the kicking
of beasts.

316.

زوجي يكذب عليّ و انا اكذب علي التجيران

*My husband tells lies to me, and I tell lies to the
neighbours.*

I do according to what I learn.

317.*

زوجي ما غار فتّش عليّ عشيقي بشمعة

*My husband was not jealous, (although) my lover
came to search for me with a candle.*

On the blindness of cuckolds.

318.*

زوج القحبه قواد بشهادته

*The husband of the harlot is a base wretch by his own
testimony.*

319.

زعيط و معيط و نطاط الحيط

Zayt and Mayt, and jumping over the wall.

This is said of a man fond of company and noisy.
Zayt and *Mayt* are words without any literal
meaning, expressing merely the noise of á busy
crowd. (See Proverb No. 146.)

320.

زامر الحّي ما يطرب

The fifer of his (own) camp does not rejoice.

The talents of a person are less admired at home than abroad.

321.

زيتنا في دقيقنا

Our oil is (mixed) with our (own) flour.

Said when a person marries his own near relation. Oil-cakes are a favourite dish with the lower classes in Egypt; the oil used is lamp-oil (زيت حار).

322.

زاد في الطنبور نغمة

He added singing to the drum.

Said when either good or bad fortune receives an addition. طنبور the small drum or tambourine which is held in one hand and beaten with the other, and is the constant companion of the women, especially of the lower classes, in their gay moments.

323.

أزَحلَق الحمار و كان من شهوة الحمار

The ass slipped (and fell); this (proceeded) from the ass driver's desire (to see a lady).

The affair was spoiled because the person entrusted with the management of it yielded to the impulse of his own passion or interest. A lady rode

upon an ass, which the driver caused to stumble and
fall, that he might obtain a sight of the fair one.
ازحلتِ used in the Egyptian dialect for زلتِ or زحلتِ
" to slip, slide, stumble, fall," &c.

———————

حرف السين

———————

324.

سالته عن ابوه فقال خالي شعيب

*I asked him about his father. " My uncle's name is
Shayb," he replied.*

Applied to those giving an answer not suited to
the question. خال is the mother's brother; عم the
father's brother.

325.

سلّموا مفاتيح البرّج للقطا

They entrusted the keys of the pigeon-house to the cat.

برج in Egypt is the name given to the pigeon-
houses, which in the open country are built in the
shape of small towers, upon a plan much resembling
that of the propylæa of the ancient temples.

326.*

سَموك راجح قال ان شا الله نجي الحق

*They have called thee Rádjeh. "If God please,"
they said, " (now) we shall come to the just
(measure)."*

Thy reputation and outward appearance promise
much. *Rádjeh* is frequently used as a man's name;
it also in the Egyptian dialect signifies "to increase
the weight of the lighter scale until it equal the
other." الحق is not only "truth," but also "just,"
and "one's own due."

327.

ساعة لقلبك و ساعة لربك

One hour for thy heart, and one hour for thy Lord.

Divide thy time between heavenly and worldly
concerns.

328.

سني و لاش و جاها النفاس

*A lean little thing of a lady; and (moreover) in
childbed.*

She was miserable enough, and still became
more miserable (by the labours of childbed). سني
used in the Egyptian dialect for ست.—و لاش is
said instead of و لاشي فيه a common expression to
denote a person or thing of utter insignificance, poor,
thin, miserable. النفاس is the state of a woman for

forty days after the birth of her child, during which time the Moslim law regards her as impure.

329.

سوق الفسوق قايم

The market of debauch is always open.

قايم "erect;" if said of the market, it means "open."

330.

سَكّ بمنفعة ما علي القفا منه منضرّة

A blow that is profitable does not hurt the neck.

331.*

سلاح حاضر و عاقل غايب

Arms ready and good sense absent.

On a passionate man ready to vent his rage.

332.*

سابق الحجّ بمرحلة

He is proceeding to the pilgrimage by a day's journey.

Said of the hasty.

333.

سوسوا السّفل بالمخالفة

Govern the rabble by opposing them.

سوسوا is the imperative of the verb ساسا—يسوس The substantive is سياسة which means the government or administration of the executive power, in

opposition to that of the judicial body or حكم الشرع
In the Egyptian dialect سياسة has also another sense,
and means " to talk gently to a person," " to coax or
wheedle him." سياسته means then, " I have talked
gently with him, enticed him by soft words." The
grooms in Egypt are called سياس (singular سايس)
because they treat (or ought to treat) the horse
gently. The proverb means, that low people can
only be governed by acting in direct opposition to
their inclinations.

334.

سلطان غشوم خير من فتنه تدوم

*A tyrannical sultán is better than constant broils (or
anarchy).*

335.

سمع الغنا برسام حاد

The hearing of music is a poignant pain.

This is said in ridicule of misers, who are reproached for their contempt of music and songs; in
proof of which the following saying is attributed to
them :

الانسان يسمع فيطرب
فينفق فيفتكر فيغتم فيهوت

*The person listens (to music), he rejoices in it, spends
money (on the songstress); then comes reflection,
he grieves and dies.*

برسام a Persian word, meaning the pain of any

disease; it is naturalized in Egypt among the physicians, and signifies a violent pain, or distemper in
the brain.

336.

سارت به الركبان

The riders have carried it with them (on their journey).

Said of a piece of news so publicly known, that
even the Bedouin travellers heard it, and reported it
in every place on their way. ركب is a party of
Bedouins mounted on horses or camels.

337.

الاستقصا فرقة

Inquiries become (or lead to) separation.

Too much inquisitiveness or curiosity about the
affairs of another may cause a disagreement and
separation.

338.*

السلطان يَعَلّم و لا يُعَلّم

The sultán teaches, and is not to be taught.

339.*

اسجد لقرد السوء في زمانه

Prostrate thyself before the wicked monkey in his
time (of power).

340.

السنور الصياح لا يصطاد شي·

The cat that is (always) crying catches nothing.

To be successful in taking game one must proceed with secrecy and caution.

حرف الشين

341.

شي ما طبخنا جانا دي الجمر من اين

We have nothing cooked; whence came this fiery coal?

On unforeseen and undeserved mishaps. جَمر
is the usual term for lighted coal. بَصَّة is employed
also in the same sense.

342.

شي ما اكلنا نشرب علي ايش

We have eaten nothing; why should we drink?

We have not done anything to render necessary
the action in question. It is usual among people
in the East to drink only after eating, so that being
thirsty they may the more enjoy the draught.
علي ايش is put here for لايش or لايشي as the prepositions علي and الي are in general used indiscrimi-

nately. Thus, تضربني علي اي "why, or for what dost thou beat me ?"

343.

شددوني حزّموني ما لي علي الحرب طاقة

They prepared me ; they girded me ; but I have not strength for war.

Notwithstanding every assistance the person is unfit for his business. شددوني from يشدّ "to make ready," "to pack up and prepare for travelling."

344.

شبيه الشي منجذبٌ اليه

It resembles the thing that is attracted towards it.

This saying, which sounds better in Arabic than in my translation, is frequently quoted, to say that a person frequents those people only whose characters agree with his own. The construction is الشي الذي منجذب اليه شبيه

345.

شكروا القط خري في بيت الدقيق

They praised the cat ; she (then went and) dirted in the meal-box.

Said of those who become insolent and over-bearing in consequence of praise.

346.

شالوه من الدقن خطّوه في الشارب

They took it off from the beard and put it into the
moustaches.

The change did not better the condition.

347.

شرا العبد و لا تربيته

The buying of a slave; but not the training of him.

The Eastern people know well how difficult a
task it is to educate a slave and break his stubborn
temper.

348.

شابت لحيته طابت عشرته

His beard became grey; his society (then) became
agreeable.

349.

شهر ما هو لك لا تعدّ ايامه

Of a month that does not belong to thee, do not count
the days.

Do not score up the profits of others which can
never become thine own. By شهر or "month," is
here understood the monthly pay or gain.

350.

شحّات من شحّات امتلات مخلاته

A beggar filled his sack from another beggar.

شحّات a corruption of شحّاز commonly used in

Egypt for "a beggar." مخلاة is the bag out of which
horses and asses get their evening allowance of barley
or beans. It is loosely tied to the mouth over the
head, like a muzzle, and the mouth and half of the
head are in the bag during the time of feeding.

351.

شرط المرافقة الموافقة

*The (first) condition of friendship is to agree with
each other.*

352.

شيب و عيب

Greyheaded and vicious.

353.＊

شماته الحساد تفقت الفواد

The rejoicing of the envious rends the heart.

354.

شرارة تحرق الحارة

A single spark can burn the whole quarter.

Trifles may cause universal disaster.

355.＊

شي. لا يشبع يجوع

A thing that does not satiate, creates hunger.

356.*

شيل بتاعك حتي احط بتاعي لا حين انا مستعاجل

Take away thine, that I may put down mine, for I am in haste.

On an angry person in haste, who thinks that every one must make room for him and give way to his desires or caprices. بتاعك and بتاعي are expressions commonly used in Egypt for "thine" and "mine." In the same manner متاعك and متاعي are used by the Moggrebíns; and the Arabians say حقك and حقي From the singular بتاع a plural is thus formed in the vulgar dialect, بتوع—and we hear الكتب بطوعه "his books," الخيل بطوعي "my horses," الولاد بطوعك "thy children."

357.

شبعت اكلاب تهادوا

The dogs became satiated, and then made presents to each other (of the remaining meat).

This is applied to the generosity evinced by páshás and other great men towards each other.

358.

شي شاط و شي باط و شي اكلنه القطاط

Part (of it) was burnt, part of it spoiled, and part eaten by the cats.

For money frivolously spent, such is the account given to him who had possessed it. قطاط a vulgar

plural of قط The term باط is used by the gardeners;
who, about Cairo, are accustomed to prick the figs
of the sycamore, while yet on the tree and before
they are ripe, with a pointed iron, so as to tear out
of them a piece, not larger than a pea; this is done
to render the fruit more sweet, for experience has
shown that an increase of sweetness is the consequence of allowing the air to enter by that operation
into the heart of the fruit. Figs that have not been
pricked never acquire a good flavour and are called
باط or spoiled. The operation itself is styled "the
circumcision of sycamore figs." تختين الجميز

359.*

شيل يدك من المرق لا تحترق

*Take off thy hand from the broth lest it should be
burnt.*

Said to expose an insidious adviser whose object
was that he might have the broth for himself.
لا تحترق in the Egyptian dialect for لئن لا تحترق In
similar cases the لئن is often dropt in conversation.

360.

شويخ و يتحالا

*A little old man, yet he plays the part of a gay
spark.*

شويخ the diminutive of شيخ.—يتحالا from حلو " to
play the spark or gallant."

361.

شاجرة تستظل بها لا تدعي بقطعها

A tree that affords thee shade, do not order it to be cut down.

362.

شيل ابوك عن اخوك

Take off thy father from thy brother.

This expression, which has no real sense in itself, has received, I know not how, a kind of meaning in the familiar language of conversation. It implies "after many difficulties," or "in short," or "to make few words," or "at last:" thus in talking of a journey they say, "we travelled, we became very tired on the road, thirst came upon us, and hunger, we had to fight—'take off thy father from thy brother'—until at last we arrived." كنا مسافرين فتعبنا في الطريق و عطشنا و جعنا و تقاتلنا شيل ابوك عن اخوك حتي وصلنا

363.

شاخاخ انحدر علي خرا قال مرحبا قرداش

Urine alighted upon dirt. "Welcome, my friend," he said.

This is to ridicule the dirty rascally Turkish soldiers, who when they meet salute each other in the Turkish manner with the expression مرحبا قرداش. "Welcome, brother, or friend!"

364.

الشر قديم

Evil is of old date.

365.

شغلني الشعير عن الشعر و البّر عن البرّ

The barley engrossed my thoughts instead of the poetry, and the corn instead of liberality.

I had things quite different in my head. This saying, which is without wit, puns in the Arabic text. شغلني عنه "it engaged my leisure or attention and prevented me from adverting to the other." This is an expression much used.

حرف الصاد

366.

صارت القوتة شاعرة

The owl has become a poetess.

Of those who undertake professions for which they are not qualified. القوتة more commonly called ام قويقة is that species of small owl which the Syrians denominate بومه

367.

صادفت الحمير التلاليس

The asses have met with the sacks.

Misfortunes return. تلاليس is the plural of تليس
(See No. 254.)

368.

صار نقّاب الغراير واعظا

*He who made a hole in the corn sacks has become a
preacher.*

A thief turned saint. نقّاب one who bores a
hole, more particularly with the intention of stealing.
Thus نقّاب الحيط signifies one who breaks through a
wall that he may steal in the house, an operation
practised with incredible dexterity by the thieves of
Upper Egypt. غراير the plural of غرارة a corn bag
carried by camels; it is shorter but wider than the
تليس In the southern parts of Syria the غرارة is a
corn measure.

369.

صام سنة و فطر علي بصلة

*He fasted for a whole year, and then broke his fast
with an onion.*

We sometimes find persons of good repute who
forfeit their character upon some trifling occasion,
or to obtain some small advantage. When the
Ramadhán is over the Moslims break their fast on

the morning of the great feast (يفطروا) with some
dainty morsels from their kitchens. It is thought
meritorious on that occasion to eat first a few dates,
after the example of Mohammed, and it would be
shameful to use so mean a thing as an onion. The
term يفطر is applied to the legal breaking of the fast,
as also to the illegal breaking of it during the course
of the month of Ramadhán ; and it is thus said of
a person هو فاطر or "he is breakfasting," when he
eats in secret, which thus becomes a very opprobrious
expression.

370.

صغار قوم كبار اخرين

*The little among (certain) people are great among
other people.*

371.*

صَلَحتَ عويشة لعبد الكريم

The little Ayshe well suited Abd el Kerym.

On the meeting of two persons who suit each
other. يصلح لي in the Egyptian dialect means "it
fits or suits me," "it is of use to me," or "proper
for me." عويشة is the diminutive of عيشة

372.

صباح الفوّال و لا صباح العطّار

*The morning salutation to the bean-seller, and not to
the druggist.*

Rather be poor but healthy like a peasant, than

rich but require the apothecary's medicines. The
word صباح is here put for مصابحة "the first meeting
or saluting on going out in the morning." According
to popular belief in the East, the good or bad luck of
the day is influenced by the object first seen on
coming out of the door in the morning. Thus it is
said if a lucky object present itself at early hours,.
صباحنا طيب "our morning salute is fortunate or
good." الفوال from فول is the man who early in the
day sells coarse horse-beans (called when boiled
مدمس) in the bázár; they form the principal breakfast of the lower classes; but it requires the stomach
of a peasant to digest them—they are mixed with
butter or lamp-oil. The druggists are at the same
time the common physicians of the town.

373.

اصاب التيس الما‟ و بل شواربه

The goat met the water and wetted his whiskers.

On a person immoderately enjoying the good
luck that had happened to him.

374.

صاحب القليل اولي به

Who possesses little has the first right to it.

375.

صاهر كراشاني جزار قال جا النخرا لباب الدار

A seller of dogs-meat became the son-in-law of a

butcher. "(There,)" they said, "the dirt has come to the gate of (its) house."

Said of a connection formed between two low fellows; it is usual to abridge this proverb and only quote the latter phrase, جا الخرا لباب الدار The person is called كراشاني who sells the كرشة or stomach of a sheep, together with tripes or entrails and all other kinds of dogs-meat; which, however, in the East, seldom falls to the lot of dogs, but is purchased by poor people.

376.

صَقَل جبّته و نَفَش حْليته

He has smoothed his cloak and cleaned his beard.

He prepared himself for the business. صقل when used on the subject of cloth, means "to pass a hot iron over it to restore its lustre:" if spoken of paper, it means "to glaze it." جبّة is the under vest of cloth as worn in the East. نفش in the Egyptian dialect "to cleanse the beard from dust;" the word سرّح is used in the same sense.

377.

صورة المودّة الصدق

The image of friendship is truth.

It is to be wished that the Egyptians would take this maxim as their guide. Truth in friendship does not occur in the East; I can at least conscientiously declare that neither in Syria nor in Egypt did any

instance of its appearing under difficult circumstances ever come within my observation : but on
the contrary, numerous cases where those who called
themselves friends, betrayed each other on the
slightest prospect of gain, or through fear, or some
other base motive.

378.

صاحب الحاجة اعمي

Who wants a thing is blind (to its·faults).

In the Egyptian dialect صاحب الحاجة means "he
who wants the thing," "who asks it," or also "he
who possesses the thing." In the first sense الحاجة
stands for الاحتياج—and صاحب الحاجة means then
the same as طالب الحاجة (See No. 34.)

379.

اصاب اليهودي لحما رخيص فقال هذا منتن

*A Jew found meat at a low price. "It stinks," he
then said.*

On the excuses offered by a miser.

380.*

صفعة بنقد خير من بدرة بنسية

*A ready blow with cash is better than eighty thousand
derhems of promised future payments.*

بدرة is equal to "eighty thousand derhems," a
term not used at present in keeping accounts. نسية
in the Egyptian dialect equivalent to اجل or وعد

حرف الصّاد

381.

ضراط الابل و لا تسبيح اسمك

Rather (hear) the flatulencies of the camels, than the
prayers of the fishes.

The most fatiguing journey by land is preferable
to the pleasantest sea voyage. "Take thy passage
by sea," said a person to his friend, "thou wilt
see many fishes about the ship performing their
devotions." "No," replied the friend, "I think it
better to hear," &c. The Egyptians dislike sea
voyages so much that most of them choose the
tedious and fatiguing journey by land to Mekka,
rather than the shorter passage by sea. تسبيح is the
prayer سبحان الله and in general any homage paid to
the divinity.

382.

ضربتين في الراس توجع

Two blows on the head cause pain.

Said of a person who has been twice cheated in
the same manner.

383.

ضحكوا علي السقا حسبوا من حقا

They laughed with the water-carrier, he thought it to be true.

On the credulity with which inferiors listen to the joking promises of their superiors. ضحكوا علي usually means "they laughed *at* him;" but sometimes, as here, "they laughed *with* him," or "joked with him." حسبوا the Egyptian pronunciation of حسبه having the last syllables very strongly accented, thus "*hasabōoe.*"

384.

ضيف الكرام يضيّف

The guest of the hospitable treats hospitably.

Or he learns hospitality from those who have evinced it towards him. This alludes to a custom general in the East; a man invited by any respectable person to an entertainment may bring with him several of his own friends without the desire or permission of the host; who, nevertheless, treats them with as much politeness as those whom he had himself particularly invited.

385.

سربني و بكّي و سبقني و شكي

He beat me and cried out; he got the start of me and complained.

Said of those who complain in the midst of their successes.

386.

ضيف البدوي يسرق ثيابك

Entertain the Bedouin, he will steal thy clothes.

On ingratitude. The Bedouins of Egypt have the worst reputation amongst the townspeople; and many of them, reduced to a mongrel race between free Bedouins and peasants, have adopted all the vices of the latter. ضيف is the Egyptian imperative of ينضيف "to treat as a guest," "to entertain."

387.

ضرب الحبيب مثل اكل زبيب

A blow from our lover is as (sweet as) the eating of raisins.

Here the wit lies merely in the Arabic rhyme of *zebyb*, raisin, with *habyb*, lover.

388.

ضاربني و لا تمسك خصاي

Fight with me, but do not lay hold of such a part as may be seriously injured.

Observe some decency and moderation in thy enmity. When the Egyptian peasants fight with each other it frequently happens that the weaker seizes his adversary in such a manner as to cause dangerous or fatal results.

389.

ضاع عقله في طولة

His understanding is lost in his length.

Said of a person as tall in stature as he is stupid in mind.

390.

ضحك الجوزة بين الحجرين

(Like) the laughter of the nut (when cracked) between two stones.

Said of smiles or laughter forced amidst poignant sufferings.

391.

ضع الامور وواضعها تضعك موضعك

Put the things into their places, they will put thee into thy place.

Give to every one his due and right, and thou shalt have thy due. This saying also means, "make no innovations, and thou shalt not be disturbed."

392.

اضرب البري حتي يعترف المجتري

Strike the innocent, that the guilty may confess.

What a judicial maxim! It is related that in an intricate law suit, the kadhy caused a person avowedly innocent to be bastinadoed. When the poor man complained, the kadhy declared that he beat him merely with the hope that whoever was the real culprit might be induced to confess out of compassion.

393.

ضحك الافاعي في جراب النورة

(Like) the laughter of serpents in the sack of burning chalk.

This in purport is similar to No. 390. To torment serpents the children put them into a sack of unslaked lime, and then pour water on it; the hisses of the serpents while they suffer the torture of burning, are called by the children "the laughing of the serpents." نورة is unextinguished lime; the same name is also given to a paste made of this lime and mercury, which is used in the bath as a depilatory to remove hairs from the body.' جراب is a "leather bag."

394.

ضيق الحوصلة

(He is) of narrow throat.

This is said of a person who blabs every secret. حوصلة in Egypt signifies that part of a bird's throat wherein the food is deposited before digestion.

395.*

اضبط من الاعمي

(He) holds faster than the blind man.

Said of one who never relaxes his hold. Blind men grasp at the objects before them with peculiar force and eagerness.

396.

اضيق من سمّ الخياط

Narrower than the ear of a needle.

Applied to business of a difficult nature. سمّ الخياط
is an expression meaning the "ear of a needle." We
find in the Koran حتي يلج الجمل في سمّ الخياط
"until the camel shall enter into the needle's ear."

حرف الطآء

397.

طار طيرك و اخذه غيرك

Thy bird flew away, and another took it.

Another has seized upon thy good luck, or of the
opportunity that thou hast missed.

398.*

طرطوري يقع من لَطشة

(Like) a high cap, it falls off at a single blow.

This is said of an effeminate cowardly person
طرطور or طرطوري (See No. 194.) In the Egyptian
dialect لطشة signifies a blow not very violent.

399.

طبّل طَبلك و زَمّر زَمرك

Beat thy drum and blow thy pipe.

Thou hast obtained thy wishes, now rejoice, this
is the time for mirth. The Egyptians frequently
quote this saying. The drum and the pipe are
instruments much used, especially among the peasants.

400.

طيّر طيره و راح يجري خَلفه

*He caused his bird to fly away, and then went
running after it.*

On inconsistency of conduct.

401.

طَلَع نَقَبه علي شونة

The hole (which he made) opened into a granary.

Said of the failure of a person's eager endeavours.
A thief contrived to make a hole in a wall, expecting
to find a room full of valuable goods on the other
side ; but instead of it he found a magazine of straw
or corn that was of little service to him. نقب is
the hole made in the wall. شونة is an open yard
where the corn or straw belonging to government is
kept. In every town of Egypt there is such a yard,
where the corn is heaped up, but uncovered and
exposed to rain ; which, however, only spoils the
surface to the depth of six or eight inches. As far

as I know, there exists at present in Egypt but one
roofed magazine of corn : this was lately erected at
Alexandria by Mohammed Aly Páshá.

402.

طالب المال بلا مال كحامل الماء في الغربال

*Who seeks for wealth without (previous) wealth is like
him who carries water in a sieve.*

403.*

طاعة اللسان ندامة

Obedience to the tongue (causes) repentance.

Who leaves his tongue uncontrolled, repents.

404.

طبيب يداوي الناس و هو عليل

*(Like) a physician curing the people, while he himself
is distempered.*

(A verse.)

405.

طعمة الاسد تخمة الذيب

The food of the lion (causes) indigestion to the wolf.

تخمة surfeit, indigestion.

406.

الطمع الكاذب يدق الرقبة

False ambition severs the neck.

It leads to perdition.   طمع means "avidity,"

whether for pecuniary gain, or for power, or fame,
in which latter sense it means " ambition." يدق in
the Egyptian dialect, " to strike," " to cut off," &c.

حرف الظآء

407.

ظلم البهايم حرام

The ill-treatment of brute creatures is unlawful.

408.

ظنان خوان بعيد الاحسان

Suspicious, treacherous, remote from good works.

Striking characteristics of a worthless person.
ظنان is one who thinks ill of others, because it is
understood الذي يظن بالسوء

409.

ظلوم غشوم كعب الشؤم

Tyrannical, cheating, of bad omen.

كعب السؤم means that his *heel* (and therefore
the whole person) is of bad omen : it stands for
كعبه شؤم The Egyptians say concerning a thing
which is of bad omen to its possessor كعبه عليه
موش طيب " his heel is not good for it," or " his

heel in passing over it will be unlucky." (موش
for (ما هو شي) With respect to bad omens the
Egyptians say اعتاب و اكعاب و نواصي " thresholds,
heels, and the horses' forelocks;" meaning that
houses, men, and horses, are most exposed to the
evil eye and bad omens. This is probably derived
from the saying of Mohammed, ان يكون الشوُم نفي
ثلاث الدار و المراة و الدابة " Let the bad omen reside
only in three things; the house, the woman, and
the animal." The ancient Arabs were extremely
superstitious on this subject; and even now the fear
of a bad omen is universal, and pervades every
transaction.

حرف العين

410.

عين لا تري قلب لا يكحزن

(*When*) *the eye does not see, the heart does not grieve.*

Be not an eye-witness of misfortunes.

411.

علي قد الكسا مدّ رجليك

*In proportion to the (length of) thy garment stretch
out thy legs.*

Accommodate thyself to the circumstances in

which thou art placed. To stretch out one's leg beyond the cloak, so that any part of it should appear, is reckoned highly indecent and unmannerly among respectable persons in Eastern society. Before a superior the man who sits cross-legged must endeavour to hide even his feet and toes, in fact he must show no part of his body but the face. In the Egyptian dialect قد is often used for قدر

412.

عدوّي غاسلتي

My enemy is the washer of my corpse.

I am thrown upon the mercy of my enemy. الغاسلة is the woman who washes the corpses of females previously to interment.

413.

عريان باسته و البخور تحته

Naked about his hinder parts, and perfume under them.

Although he has not money wherewith to purchase drawers, yet he has the vanity to perfume his hinder parts; while even the rich are content to perfume their beards. The vanity of living beyond one's station, and affecting airs of greatness, is very common among the Easterns of a low class; while on the contrary, those of the higher classes endeavour to conceal their wealth by living as poorly as is compatible with their rank.

414.

عُقلا ما اختصموا

Wise men do not quarrel with each other

415.

عداوة العاقل و لا صاحبة التجاهل

The enmity of the wise, rather than the friendship of the fool.

416.

عند المخاضة يبان الغليط

At the ford over the river the kaīyt becomes conspicuous.

On certain occasions the bad qualities of a person must show themselves. مخاضة is a fording place where the water is shallow. The peasants in crossing over hold up their loose skirts, and on such occasions the kalyt (see No. 157,) becomes conspicuous.

417.

عند الشويَ لفّ لفّ و عند لتخل انا ضرسان

At the roasted meat " take, take;" but at the vinegar " my teeth ache."

He eagerly eats the roasted meat; but when vinegar is offered he says, "it makes my teeth ache." لفّ "to encircle, to cover, or wrap up." Here it means to wrap up the pieces of roast meat in some bread as is practised at dinners in the East, where

every morsel taken from the dish is accompanied to
the mouth with a piece of bread ; or, if possible,
wrapped up in it. ضرسان is that unpleasant sensation
of the teeth when we see anything repugnant to our
nature or taste.   Vinegar made of dates is used by
the lower classes in summer ; they dip their bread
into it.

418.

عند البطون تذهب العقول

When the stomach is concerned, wisdom withdraws.

Wisdom is overpowered by hunger or dire necessity.

419.

عند المضيق لا اخ و لا صديق

*At the narrow passage there is no brother and no
friend.*

In dangerous cases we must only think of saving
ourselves.   المضيق "a narrow pass," "a difficult
moment."

420.

عيا تحفف مجنونة

A blind woman shaves an insane one.

On improper persons employed in ridiculous
affairs. تحفف is derived from حف or تحفيف " the
rubbing the skin of the face with the *libán shámy* as
a depilatory to remove hairs.   The *libán shámy*
(لبان شامي) is a white shining gum of a glutinous

quality, a kind of turpentine that is imported into
Egypt from the islands of the Archipelago, particularly from Scio, where it is produced from a species
of fir. It is used in a melted state, the finger being
dipped into it and rubbed over the face, by which
process all the hair to which it sticks is eradicated.
The women of Cairo whose beauty is obscured by
hair on the skin, avail themselves of this تحفيف

421.

علي عينك يا تاجر

To thy eye, O Merchant.

The whole is displayed before thee, therefore *open
thy eyes,* for if thou art cheated in the business, it is
now thy own fault.

422.

علي بخت زفافي قصر الليل و تابت المغاني

*To the good luck of my wedding festivities the night
was short, and the female singers became penitents.*

This is said ironically to express that the wedding
did not succeed well; and the saying is applied to
any unfortunate circumstance that throws obstacles
in the way of rejoicings. زفاف is the plural of زفة
" the procession in which the bride is carried to the
house of her spouse;" and it also signifies " the whole
wedding feast," the principal rejoicings of which take
place during the night; and at Cairo always on the
night preceding the consummation of matrimony,

which last night is called ليلة الدُخلة While I am
writing this, the whole quarter of the city in which
I reside is illuminated on a similar occasion; and
two men, one disguised as a French soldier, the
other dressed up as a French woman, play their
tricks before a large assembly of Arabs, in front of
the bridegroom's house; a third Arab personifies a
cowardly Turkish soldier making love to the lady;
he, as well as the French pair, pronounce Arabic
according to their supposed native idioms, a circumstance which causes roars of laughter. The mock-
lady's heart is won by the Turkish soldier, whose
pockets are full of gold; but the French soldier beats
the Turk unmercifully whenever he meets him, and
at last obliges him to put on his hat instead of the
turban. The female singers are mostly public women
of a loose description; those who were expected at
the wedding feast suddenly felt symptoms of repentance (تابت), and therefore did not attend.

As certain customs usual on a Moslim wedding
ceremony at Cairo have not been mentioned by former
travellers, I shall here give some account of them.
When a girl is to be asked in matrimony, a friend or
relation, or the sheikh of the young man, (who has
instructed him in reading the Korán,) goes to the
girl's father, and makes a bargain for her. It is a
real bargain, for the girl's affections are never consulted, and the amount of the price to be paid for
her (حق البنت as they call it,) is the only matter
taken into consideration, provided the stations in life
of both parties sufficiently correspond; but even in

this respect the Egyptians are not very scrupulous,
and a man of low extraction and profession who
possesses wealth often marries into a high class. The
price paid for the girl to her father, or, if he be dead,
to the nearest male relation, varies according to her
rank, fortune, or reputation for beauty. Among the
first-rate merchants the price is from two hundred to
three hundred dollars; among those of the second
class, from sixty to eighty; and the lower classes
often pay no more than from three to five dollars.
It is usual to pay half of the money immediately
in advance, this sum becomes the property of the
father; the other half remains in the bridegroom's
hands, and reverts to his wife if he should die or
divorce her; but if she herself sues for a divorce she
forfeits her claim to the money. On the day of
betrothing (يوم الخطبة) the girl's father gives a small
entertainment in his house, where none assemble but
intimate friends, the bridegroom himself not being
present. The day for the marriage is then fixed.
If any festivity is to take place (a circumstance with
which the poorer classes generally dispense), the
street wherein the bridegroom resides is for six or
seven days before the marriage decorated with flags
and various-coloured lamps, suspended from cords
drawn across the street. Three days before the
marriage ceremony the festivities usually begin; if
the parties are great and rich people, they begin
eight days before—the house is then full of company
every night, and an open table is kept. But on the
great night of the feast (that immediately preceding

the nuptial night,) singing and dancing women are
hired to attend, and the whole street is illuminated.
Next morning when the nuptials are to take place
(يوم الدّخلة), (which in Egypt is always on Monday
or Thursday, the other days being considered of bad
omen with regard to weddings,) the girl's father
repairs to the bridegroom's house, accompanied by
some of his friends, in order to conclude the marriage
compact (العقد); after a plentiful dinner the mutual
friends assemble in a circle, the girl's father and the
bridegroom sitting in the midst. The former takes
the other's hand, and after the recital of a short
prayer addresses him in these words : " I give to thee
my daughter N ٭ ٭ ٭, the adult virgin, in marriage
according to the law of God and of his prophet."
(زوجتك بنتي فلانة البكرة البالغة بسنة الله و رسوله عليه
السلام) To which the other replies : " I take thy
daughter N ٭ ٭ ٭ in marriage, the adult virgin, according to the law of God and of his prophet." The
father asks, " Dost thou accept my daughter ?"
(اقبلت بنتي) The answer is, " I have accepted her."
(قبلتها) The father immediately adds, " God bless
thee with her." (الله يبارك لك فيها) And the bridegroom replies, " I hope in God that she may prove a
blessing." (مبروك ان شاء الله) The *Fatha* (or first
chapter of the Koran) is then recited by the whole
company, and all present shake hands with the
bridegroom, and congratulate him. No document or
marriage contract is written on this occasion, nor
even at the time of betrothing, when two witnesses
only are required, to attest verbally the betrothing

and the payment of the money. While this ceremony
is taking place, the bride, having left her own house,
and accompanied by all her female relations, proceeds
through the town in a manner faithfully represented
in a plate of Niebuhr's Travels. She is completely
veiled, generally with a Cashmere shawl; a large
canopy of red silk or cotton stuff, held by four men,
is carried over her head; the musicians go before
her. She parades through all the principal streets
from morning till evening, for six or eight hours.*
When great people marry, these processions are conducted upon a more magnificent scale. I have seen
many nuptial processions of persons high in office at
the court of Mohammed Aly; the bride was seated
in a carriage, and all the different trades and professions of the town appeared personified upon richly
decorated open waggons drawn by horses; in these
waggons the tradesmen and artists had established
their shops, and sat working in the same manner as
in their own regular abodes: sixty or seventy of
those waggons followed the carriage of the bride.
Before them went rope-dancers, harlequins, &c., and
at their head was a masqued figure that is frequently
seen parading in front of nuptial processions of an
inferior order, and conducted with much less pomp
and splendour; this figure is a young man whose
head, arms, legs, and entire body are patched over

* In Syria, where this procession is accompanied with other
ceremonies and usually takes place in the early part of the night,
it is reckoned a very bad omen to pass with the bride before a
public bath, and therefore those streets are carefully avoided into
which the baths open.

with white cotton, so that no part of the skin can be
perceived, his person appearing as if completely pow-
dered over.   He exhibits, in the natural position,
that object which constituted the distinguishing
attribute of the ancient Roman god of the gardens ;
this is of enormous proportion, two feet in length,
and covered with cotton; and he displays it with
indecent gesticulation in all the bázárs before the
staring multitude, and during the whole time of the
procession.   How this custom, which is not known
in other places, began among the Egyptians, I am
unable to ascertain ; but it seems not improbably
some remnant of the worship paid by their forefathers
to that god, whose temple at Karnak is the most considerable now existing in Egypt.   Towards evening
the bride arrives, half fainting from fatigue, before
the gate of her spouse's dwelling, from which he
issues, suddenly clasps her in his arms as if by
violence, and running off with his fair prize carries
her into the female's apartments up stairs, where all
the women of both families are assembled.   This
evening is past with much fewer festivities than the
last ; there are not any public rejoicings in the
streets, and none but the relations and intimate
friends attend at supper.   The bridegroom now in
his turn leaves the house, he parades in his newest
clothes, by the light of torches and to the sound of
drums, a short way through the town, accompanied
by his friends ; he then goes to the Mosque, and
recites the *Aeshe*, or last evening prayer, after which
he returns to his home.   As soon as he enters the

house his friends leave him, but at parting strike
him many times with their hands upon his back;
these blows he endeavours to avoid by running in as
fast as possible. He is indulged with a short repose
in his own apartment, and a message is then sent
informing him that his bride is ready to receive him.
He finds her in his bedchamber, sitting upon the
sofa with two women by her side, usually the mother
or aunt, and the old midwife of her family. It is
here that for the first time her face is seen by the
bridegroom, and his expectations are but too often
disappointed. At his entrance the veil that covers
her is removed by her attendants; she then rises
and kisses his hands. An invariable and indispen-
sable custom now obliges the bridegroom to give
money to both the female attendants, and likewise to
put some money into the hands of his bride, this is
called "the price for the uncovering of the face"
(حتى كشف الوجه). If his circumstances allow him,
he generally gives gold coins : if he is poor, he gives
a piastre, or even a few paras; something, however,
must be given, although a trifling sum, in testimony
of the veil having been removed with the girl's
consent. The two women then retire, and none
remain but the bride and bridegroom. During this
first nuptial "tête à tête" many women assemble
before the door, striking drums, singing, and shouting
loudly, to prevent from being heard any conversation
that might pass between the newly married couple.
On this occasion the bridegroom must convince himself that no man has anticipated him in the possession

of the fair one, whom also he must no longer allow
to boast of being a maiden (انه يخرتها). The mode
in which he acquires that conviction is sometimes so
repugnant to manly feelings, that I must describe it
in a language better adapted than the English to a
detail of similar proceedings. انها كثيرين من الناس
تستغني في ذلك الوقت عن وطية البنت فيخرتوها باصبعهم
و العامة يستعملوا ايضا مفتاح خشب حتي الفلاحين و
ناس السفلا لا يخرتوا البنت الا بالمفتاح بل يعيبوا كل الذين
ما يفعلوا كذلك Before the bridegroom approaches
his bride it is reckoned proper that he should
utter aloud these words of the Koran: نصر من الله و
فتح قريب Among the lower classes of Moslims at
Cairo it is customary that on the day after the
nuptials certain female relations of the bride should
carry her innermost garment (not her handkerchief
as some travellers have related,) in triumph to the
houses of their neighbours. But this practise is
not adopted by the more respectable inhabitants,
among whom the chemise is exhibited only in the
bridegroom's house to the women assembled there;
and in many instances the people of high rank con-
demn even this exhibition as indecent, and no longer
allow it. On that night, immediately after the
conclusion of their first interview, the bride and
bridegroom retire to separate apartments; next
morning they go to the bath; and for seven days
after some female relations constantly remain with
the bride in the house of her husband, but he is not
permitted to approach her.

The bride furnishes herself with clothes for the marriage, and with ornaments; she brings likewise to her husband's house much furniture, bedding, kitchen utensils, &c. (called فراش) often of greater value than the price which was paid for her; those articles continue her property.

If a widow marries, none of those ceremonies take place; the nuptials are celebrated in a quiet manner by the family alone. Even the marriage of a virgin is sometimes not accompanied by any festivities, but for this omission an express stipulation must be made at the time of betrothing; else the bride and her friends would consider themselves insulted.

It is always expected that those who are invited to nuptials should bring some presents; sugar, coffee, and wax candles, are the articles generally sent on such occasions to the bridegroom's house, upon a large board covered with a fine handkerchief.

Divorces are extremely common at Cairo; I believe there are few individuals who have not divorced one wife. Polygamy is much less frequent than Europeans imagine. Of one hundred married men in this city there certainly is not more than one who has two wives; and not more than one in five hundred who has more than two. The privilege of having four, which the Moslim law allows, is enjoyed by the richest class only, those who can afford to keep separate establishments.

To estimate the condition of the Arab women at Cairo, by that reported to exist at Constantinople

and in the large Turkish towns, would be very
erroneous. Females probably enjoy more freedom
here at Cairo than in any other part of the Turkish
empire, the deserts excepted; and whether for that
reason, or from some accessory causes, they are of less
reserved manners, and more addicted to debauchery
than the women of the neighbouring countries, Syria
and Hedjáz.

423.*

عُمر الكذّاب قصير

The liar is short-lived (soon detected).

424.

علي المؤذّن ان يؤذّن

It is the business of the Mueddin to call to prayers.

There are appropriate persons for the performance
of every business. علي sometimes means "the business
of," "belonging to." Thus it is said, هذا علي "this
is my business or duty to perform," "this obligation
devolves upon me."

425.

عيش يا حمار حتي ينبت النوار

Live, thou ass, until the clover sprouts up.

Exhorting a foolish person to be patient and not
to despond, as it is quite certain that circumstances
will change for the better.

426.

علموني كيف اهاجركم قالوا خلّينا و روح

Teach me how I can depart from you. Let us alone,
they said, and begone.

Said of a person fondly imagining that he is dear
to people who do not care about him.

427.*

عاشر المصلّي تصلّي و عاشر المغنّي تغنّي

Live with him who prays, and thou prayest ; live with
the singer, and thou singest.

428.*

عفاشة و تلاشة و بقبقة وحاشة

A miserable disorderly slut talks proudly and affects
prudery.

عفاشة comes from the term عفش—which in the
Egyptian dialect signifies " miserable baggage,"
" trumpery ;" thus they say عفش نفش meaning a
" deal of rubbish and trumpery." The word نفش is
a cant term employed only in this phrase, and
without any real signification, but it serves to rhyme
with عفش (See No. 146 and No. 319.) In a wider
sense عفش means also " baggage in general," " par-
cels of goods." تلاشة from the word متلاشي " thrown
about," " disorderly," " worthless." بقبقة an imitative
word expressing the gurgling sound which water
produces in passing through the narrow opening of

earthen jars when poured out. From this is derived
its figurative sense, the talking loud, and also bab-
bling. وحاشة from يوحش "to abstract one's self
from society," "to neglect one's friends," "to behave
towards them with reserve and affected airs."

429.

عمي القط و كان بشهوة الفار

*The cat became blind yet still was hankering after
mice.*

430.

عمارة البيت و لا خرابه

*To keep the family in good condition, not to destroy
it.*

When the words عمارة and خرابة refer to بيت (a
house or family), عمارة means "to keep the family in
a good state by letting the mother live with her
husband and children;" and خرابة means "to ruin
the family by divorcing the mother and obliging her
to quit the house." خرب البيت is likewise used
when the father of a family dies.

431.

عازب و يضارب ما يخلّي له صاحب

Unmarried, quarrelsome, and retaining no friend.

Said of one whose manners are repulsive.

432.

عريان و في كمه ميزان

(Half) naked and a balance in his hand.

Miserable, still laying claim to the habits of the wealthy. عريان does not here properly mean "naked," but "half-naked," "in rags." The substantial merchants of Cairo frequently carry a small balance in their wide sleeves, to weigh the sequins and other gold coins which they receive in payment.

433.

علمناه الشحاتة سبقنا علي الابواب

We taught him begging, and (now) he has the start of us at the gates.

The pupil excelling his master. See No. 350, for شحاتة

434.

عصيدة من طبيخ ام علي

A pap of the cookery of Om Aly.

To express a thing prepared with great care and nicety. عصيدة is a pap made of meal, butter, and water, much used among the negroes and also among the peasants. ام علي a woman's name; as women are often called by the name of their favourite child, usually the first-born son.

435.*

عيبت القدر علي المغرفة قالت يا سودة يا محارفة

*The kettle reproached the kitchen spoon. "Thou
blackee," he said, "thou idle babbler."*

Of those who reprove others for faults of which
they themselves are more guilty. المغرفه is a large
wooden kitchen spoon. يحارف has not in Egypt
always the literal signification, but means "to talk
idly," "to give bad advice," "to delude a person by
shrewd words."

436.

عواض خطوطك و الحمرة امسحي عماشك يا بظرة

*Instead of thy (fine) tattoo and thy painting, wipe
off the dirt from thy face, thou hussey.*

Do what is right and necessary before thou
thinkest of what is merely ornamental. خطوط so is
called the tattooing of the female peasants and those
of the lower classes in general; this is produced by
incisions made along the forehead and temples, dis-
posed in separate lines, but never forming any regular
figures. الحمرة is the red colour, with which the gay
women paint their hands and feet; it is made either
of Henna or of Cinnabar. In the Egyptian dialect
عماش means "dirt in the eye," (and likewise, "sore-
ness of the eye"). بظرة is an insulting expression,
equivalent to "slut or wench." It originally signifies
—labia pudendorum, quæ a Cahirinis etiam زنبور
dicuntur, et in puellis exciduntur.

437.

عناق الاجتماع اطيب من عناق الوداع

The embrace at meeting is better than that at parting.

438.

عينه في الطبق و اذنه لِمَن زعق

His eye upon the cupboard, his ear towards the crier
(of things for sale in the street).

Applied to a greedy glutton. طبق is a board or
shelf in a room whereon eatables, especially fruits and
sweetmeats, are deposited. لمن زعق "to him who
cries," *viz.*, cries victuals, fruit, &c., for sale; it is
here put for في من زعق

439.

عين الشمس لم تتغطّي

The eye of the sun cannot be hidden.

Superior excellence or beauty will become known,
notwithstanding every effort made to conceal them.
عين الشمس and شمس are often said indifferently; it
also means the body of the sun, or the solar rays.
This proverb is taken from a poem in praise of wine,
beginning with the following verses :—

الراح المدام القرقف البكر العاجوز الشمطا
غطّوها الندامة قالت عين الشمس لم تتغطّيَ

In the first line there are six different terms
expressing wine.

440.

عير و استعير هذا هو العار الكـ

Borrow and lend out (what thou hast borrowed), that is the great shame.

This is a verbal play on the different meanings of عير and عار

441.

عُرس و في طرفه خِتان

A wedding, and by its side a circumcision (feast).

A surplus or superabundance of rejoicings. The term طهارة is more commonly used in Egypt than ختان To save expense the Egyptians frequently celebrate these two festivals at the same time, when an opportunity of doing so presents itself.

442.

عين القِلادة و راس التخت و أوّل التجريدة و نكتة المسألة و بيت القصيدة

The jewel of the necklace, the canopy of the throne, the vanguard of the army, the point in discourse, the best verse of the poem.

The "eye of the necklace" (عين القلادة) is the precious stone, or medallion, or gold coin, which hangs upon the breast, from the middle of a woman's necklace, to attract particular notice. تجريدة or جريدة "an army or large body of troops in actual warfare;" thus, التجريدة علي الوهابي "the army against the

Waháby." اول الجريدة is the "head or vanguard of the army, composed of the bravest soldiers." نكتة المسألة " the very point or most material part of the question under discussion." بيت القصيدة so is styled the verse (بيت) wherein the poet has exerted his utmost powers; the main verse of the poem, usually found towards the end of those compositions called *Kasýde*.

443.

عصارة لُوم في قارورة خَبث

A dirty liquor in a wretched bottle.

A bad character and unseemly body. عصارة a liquid extracted by pressure from whatever source it may be. قارورة the same as قزازة a "glass bottle."

444.

عليه ما علي الطبل يوم العيد

May that come upon him which comes upon the drum on the feast-day.

Much beating; verbatim, "to him what to the drum on the day of festival."

445.

عليه ما علي المحصنات من العذاب

May those torments be his which are the due of the adulteresses.

May he suffer stoning. Here is to be understood المحصنات الزانيات or those women whom the Koran condemns to be stoned (ترجم).

446.

عليه ما علي اصحاب السبت

May that be his lot which is the lot of the Sabbat men.

The *Sabbat* men, or the Jews, are doomed to hell fire by the Koran. All these imprecations are in common and frequent use.

447.

الاعمي يتخري فوق السطم و يظن ان الناس لا يروه

The blind man does what is nasty upon the roof of the house, and thinks that the people do not see him.

Said of a blockhead who fancies that the world is unacquainted with his foolish tricks, however openly he practises them. The meaning of فوق السطم is properly " *above* the roof or terrace of the house;" but it is constantly used to express " *upon* the terrace."

448.

العادة تومُّ الطبيعة

Custom is the twin of the innate character.

(See No. 133.)

449.

اعز من مِّخ البعوض

More rare than fly-brains.

Said of any thing very scarce.   بعوض means

originally (as here) "a fly"; but in the common dialect of Egypt this name is given to a sort of vermin that stick to the beards of filthy peasants, and are also called صيبان

450.

اعز من انف الاسد

Scarcer than the nose of the lion.

Said of a rare thing, because it is difficult to take a lion by the nose.

451.

اعلق من قراد

More adhesive than a tick.

Said of a person whom one cannot shake off. قُراد is a species of tike (or tick); these creatures attach themselves firmly to the body (especially to the belly) of a camel, and annoy him extremely.

452.

اعدل من الميزان

More just than a balance.

453.

العز في نواصي الخيل

Honour (resides) in the manes of horses.

This is taken from the saying of Mohammed, الخير معقود بنواصي الخيل and is often quoted to show the superior distinction which a horseman claims above him who rides upon an ass. نواصي properly

signifies the lock of hair that falls on the horse's
forehead.

454.

عَذر لم يتولَّي الحَق نسجه

*It is an excuse the texture of which is not truth's own
work.*

Said of a false excuse. The construction is الحَق
يتولَّي لم يتولَّي نسج هذا العُذر In the Egyptian dialect
often means "to do a thing by one's self," " by one's
own labour," equivalent to الفعل بالنفس—نسج or ينسج
"to weave." A more common term for weaving is
قَزر and a weaver is called قَزار in Egypt.

حرف الغين

455.

غابت السباع و لعبت الضباع

The lions withdrew, the hyænas then played.

A verse which is frequently quoted conveys the
same meaning :

و اذا خلا الميدان من اسدٍ
رقص ابن عِرسٍ و زمزم النَّمِس

And when the lion has cleared the field,
The ferret dances and the Ichneumon sings.

ابن عِرس or عِرس is a species of small weasel or

ferret very common in Egypt ; it comes into the houses, feeds upon meat, is of a gentle disposition although not to be domesticated, and full of play and gambols. النمس is the Ichneumon rat, that has a sharp shrill voice. زم زم in the Egyptian dialect, means " to sing," " to recite a poem."

456.

غرامة بيّنة و لا ربح بطي

A clear loss rather than a profit of distant expectation.

457.

غلَا و سَو كيل

Scarcity and bad (corn) measuring.

Bad times and bad men.

458.

غراب قال الله قال الله حتى قال بقي نبّاش التخرا واعظ

A crow exclaimed " God is the truth ;" " then," quoth one, " the dirt scraper has become a preacher."

بقي is a kind of expletive often used in Egypt, sometimes meaning "there," "therefore," "altogether," or " in short ;" but at other times it has not any sig-nification whatever and is quite superfluous. (See No. 263.) ينبش " to search upon the ground," " to dig it slightly," " to scrape, or scratch it."

459.

غلام كفاية لا جامكية و لا جراية

A boy-servant of all work, without food or wages.

Said in reference to the unwillingness of a person
to reward those who have served him well. كفاية
"sufficient," *i.e.*, for all the work required in the
house. جامكية is the common term in Egypt for
wages or monthly pay. جراية in the Egyptian dialect
signifies the daily allowance of victuals given to
soldiers, labourers, servants, &c.

460.

غيرة القحبة زنا و غيرة الحرّة بكا

*The jealousy of the harlot (is evinced by) adultery,
that of the virtuous woman (by) weeping.*

461.

غَبن الصديق و لا مصاحبة العدو

*Anger with our friend, rather than constant friend-
ship with our enemy.*

غَبن " to be angry with," "to quarrel with." The
expression انا مغبون منه "I am angry with him," is
often heard.

462.

غدوة في الصعيد ما هي بعيد

The dinner is in Upper Egypt—it is not far off.

This is said in ridicule of the parasites (طفيل) who
run from one end of the town to the other for the
sake of a good dinner.

463.

غيرة المراة مفتاح طلاقها

The jealousy of a wife is the key to her divorce.

464.

غنا بلا نقوط شبه ميّت بلا حنوط

*Singing without remuneration is like a dead body
without perfumes.*

When the singing women perform in Egypt they
collect money from all the persons present, the
landlord or host as well as the guests ; and according
to custom, one of them proclaims with a loud voice
the sum which each person puts on the plate,
mentioning at the same time the donor's name ;
this custom excites the vanity of those who form
the company, each from a kind of emulation in
liberality wishing to have his own name mentioned
as the most generous ; this heightens the interest
and pleasure of the society, and fills the pockets of
the singers. نقوط signifies the money given to the
singers by the company. حنوط is a mixture of
camphor and rose-water, with which the face of a
dead person is sprinkled before the body is placed
in the coffin.

465.

غريمي اقصر مني

*My debtor is still more backward in payment than
I am myself.*

This is said in excuse for our not paying a debt,

as our own debtor does not pay us. غريم in the
Egyptian dialect means the debtor and also the
creditor. اقصر is here used in the same sense as مقاصر
which means in Egypt one who is backward in
paying, or generally remiss in doing what is his
duty.

466.

غدّي ماخامير و لا تعشّي سكاري

*Give dinner to the drunken—but not supper to the
tipsy.*

The drunken, it is supposed, will become sober in
the evening ; but the tipsy during supper will be in-
toxicated and continue so all night. ماخمور "a man
completely drunk." ساكر or سكران "one who is
tipsy." رجل في النشوة "a person clouded or stupified
with wine," being the first stage of drunkenness.
This expression corresponds exactly to the German
"*benebelt.*"

467.

غضبه علي طرف مناخيره

His anger is on the edge of his nose.

Ever ready to burst forth. مناخير properly
signifies *nostrils*, but is used constantly in Egypt
for *nose*, or انف—a term seldom heard there in
familiar conversation.

468.

غاص غوصة و جا بروشة

*He plunged a (deep) plunge, and came up with a
piece of dung.*

حرف الفآء

469.

فار ما وسِعه شَقَّه حطّوا في قعره مِرزِبّة

*A mouse feared that her hinder part was not suffi-
ciently wide ; they then introduced an iron pestle.*

On remedies that cause an evil worse than that
for which they are applied. قعر is a low word for
طيز—دبر—شتى &c., more politely expressed by است
The word مِرزِبّة means a thick heavy iron club held
by both hands, and used by the public coffee-roasters
to pound the roasted beans in large mortars.

470.

فقما و تشرب ملوخيا

She has a distorted mouth and drinks Meloukhya.

She does a thing seldom done by others, although
she is less qualified for doing so than others. فقما
" with a distorted mouth." The pot-herb *meloukhya*
is boiled with meat till it forms a thick broth, of
which the Egyptians are very fond ; they eat it with
a spoon or dip their bread into it, but few drink the
thick broth, and the woman with a distorted mouth

has the least claim to do so, because she will probably spill it, being scarcely able to drink mere water without letting some fall about. The ا at the end of نقما and ملوخيا is according to the pronunciation of the lower classes of Cairo, by which a strong accent is laid upon the ة at the end of feminine nouns.

471.

فدَان يكرم بقصبة

A feddán may have a kassaba bestowed in its favour.

A trifling thing may be sacrificed in favour of a great one. It would have been better Arabic thus: قصبة يكرم لفدان The feddán is an Egyptian land measure, of which the extent differs according to the various departments of the revenue :

"*Feddán el kamel*," or "*el Djerkasy*," is composed of 400 square rods or *kassabas*, and is computed at 24 *kerats;* the kassaba being an imaginary portion of the division which comprises 24 kerats, and used on many occasions.

Feddán of $333\frac{1}{3}$ square kassabas or 20 kerats.

Feddán of 300 kassabas or 18 kerats; this is the feddán most used at present. The kassaba that composes it has $3\frac{64}{100}$ metres. But this kassaba, or rod, which the surveyors now use in measuring out the sown fields every year, according to the new regulations of Mohammed Ali Pasha, (who has abolished the land taxes assessed upon villages, or districts at large, and now takes throughout the country the *miri* from each feddán), this rod, I say, is often changed, *i.e.* shortened, to cheat the peasants, and every two or three years an inch is lopped off from it. The poor fellah is little aware of this diminution at the moment, but he has, however, found out that at present (in 1817) the kassaba used is only three-fourths of what it was twelve years ago under the Mamelouks, although the feddán for which they pay the tax still contains the same number of rods. The manner in which the kassaba itself is measured favours a deception of this kind. Immemorial custom has decided that it ought to consist of twenty-four fists (قبضة), meaning such as are formed in seizing a stick with the hand and keeping the thumb erect upon it, thus—

No exact measure has ever been determined, and it may be easily conceived that government does not choose the largest hands to fix the length of the rod. In 1816, the kassaba had about 6⅓ Cairo pikes. The peasants are so stupid, or so negligent, that perhaps they seldom discover the cheat, or

think it of little moment ; besides, they respect it as
a custom of their forefathers. The shortening of
the kassaba by an inch, probably makes an increase
in the receipts of the Fiscus of from £20,000 to
£30,000 sterling per annum. This is one of the
numerous tricks and secret measures by which
government curtails the fellah's pittance without
incurring the blame of open tyrannical extortion.

According to the latest data there are about
2,000,000 of feddán now under actual cultivation in
Egypt, (of which five-sixths are sown with grain).
Then 2,000,000 of feddán at the rate of $3\frac{2}{3}$ or
4 dollars annual tax per feddán, (as it may be now
computed,) gives a land revenue of at least 7,000,000
of dollars to the Pasha of Egypt; a sum that forms,
I believe, little more than half of his income.

As I have mentioned the subject of taxation in
Egypt, it may gratify the reader to lay before him
an accurate statement of the proportion which the
land tax bears to the field income of the cultivator
in this country. The following is an account of the
expenditure on a field near Esne, in Upper Egypt,
and the produce of it in winter 1813–1814. It
must be recollected that in the higher parts of
Egypt the Nile never inundates the ground, but
that the fields are irrigated in high-water time either
by means of wheels, or of buckets worked by men,
who draw the water up from the river.

A society of twenty-six peasants had hired a
piece of ground comprising seventeen feddáns, of
which fourteen were destined for durra, and three

for water-melons ; it being the custom of poor fellahs, who have not any landed property of their own, to associate every year and hire a field.

Expenses incurred in the Cultivation of Seventeen Feddáns.

For three months twenty of the associates were occupied in drawing up water from the river in buckets, which they emptied into the small channels made to convey the water into the field. This labour was continued incessantly during the whole day until the durra approached to maturity. Those who could not themselves attend, were obliged to send in their stead labourers hired for the purpose. Besides these twenty men, two were employed in keeping the channels clear of mud and weeds ; two others in partitioning the water at its issue from the channels over the field ;. and one man superintended the whole of the labourers, and excited them to exertion. The sheikh, or head man of the company, was alone exempt from contributing his share of actual work.

Piasters.

The daily labour of a fellah in drawing the bucket (which is of a more fatiguing nature than the hardest field work in Europe), was then estimated in Esne at fifteen paras, of which ten were reckoned as pay in cash, and five paras for food, (*viz.*, lentils, oil or durra cakes,) thus making the labour of each man during the three months amount to the value of thirty-four piasters ; or for the whole   850

Piasters.

After the conclusion of those three months, when the clusters of the durra (called then قناديل) were nearly ripe, five or six persons were employed in watching the crop of durra as well as the melon field, to guard them from nightly robbers, and from the multitude of sparrows and other small birds, which often, in spite of every precaution, deprive the fellah of the whole fruit of his labours. The daily pay of these men is estimated at twelve paras, or sixty for them all, during two months, until the durra harvest in February or March . .   90

For the construction of water-buckets and the poles to which they are suspended, and which facilitate the operation of drawing them up .   4

Seed (تقاوي) of 14 feddáns of durra, at one raftan per feddán, makes 3½ mud for the whole, cr   2½

Seed for three feddáns of melon field . .   1

Labour of throwing the durra seed . . .   3

Labour of planting the melon seed . . .   2

Expenses of harvest, twelve persons for four days, at fifteen paras per day   18

Expenses of treading out the grain and winnowing it, which is performed on the spot when the produce of the field is collected in a large heap   3

Hire of the ground paid by the society to the owner of the field, 1½ mud for each feddán, we may say   20

TOTAL EXPENSE attending the field labour—*piasters* . . . . . .}   993½

Produce of Seventeen Feddáns.

Piasters.

The water-melons of the three feddáns, sold in the market of Esne at from two to three paras each 280

Each of the associates for his own eating from off the field about sixty paras 40

For about three months the associates cut every day weeds and grass from the durra and melon field, which they divided among them every evening; part of the weeds and grass they sold at the market of Esne for feeding horses, camels, and asses in that town; part of them they gave to their own sheep and goats; and part was taken away from them forcibly every morning, by the soldiers of the garrison. The daily share of each associate may be computed at from six to seven paras, making for the three months about fifteen piasters per head 390

When the grain was divided every associate carried home four and-a-half *tellys*, or forty *mud soogy*, worth at that time thirty-two paras per mud, or thirty-two piasters for the share of each; in all 832

The dry durra stalks, which after the harvest fall to the share of each individual, and of which the leaves are given to the cattle as food in the summer months, the canes of them being used for fuel or for thatching, were worth about four piasters; or in the whole 104

Piasters.

Each associate besides fattened at home with the dry durra leaves a couple of sheep, which he could sell afterwards with a profit of about three piasters per head ; we may say six piasters for each individual ; or in the whole . 156

TOTAL PRODUCE of the field—*piasters* 1802

I must here observe that the durra harvest had been bad, because a high wind and heavy rain in November had bent or broken the stalks of the plant ; otherwise the produce of the field might have been 1000 piasters in durra, instead of 832 ; the water having been very abundant this year.   However, two or three years seldom elapse without some calamity equally distressing as heavy rain ; either innumerable flights of birds, worms in the ground, or low water, which adds considerably to the labour and expense of irrigation, are circumstances that cause a great diminution in the produce : for those misfortunes, if the crop does not entirely fail, government never makes the smallest allowance.

Piasters.

Total produce	1802
Total expense	993½
Clear produce	808½

The taxes of this year were twenty-nine piasters per each feddán of durra and melons, which are usually sown together, making in all 493

Remained to the fellahs, taxes deducted ⎱
—*piasters* . . . . ⎰   315½

The income of a feddán (taxes deducted) was therefore 18½ piasters.

Each of the associates had for his share twelve piasters, after having worked during the whole winter season. As the durra fields are very seldom (if ever) sown twice in Upper Egypt, the man had to support himself during the rest of the year either by joining some other society to sow summer seed, or by hiring himself out as a labourer.

The produce of the corn field is better, although the seed produces much less, because corn does not require such long continued or incessant labour of irrigation. At the same period, the produce of a corn field near Esne, was 84 piasters per feddán; the expenses may be calculated at 15 piasters, and the taxes laid upon corn fields were then 40½ piasters; there remained a clear profit of 29 piasters.

The corn measures of Upper Egypt are the *erdeb* and the *tellys*. The *erdeb* has 12 *muds*, or 24 *kadahs*, or 48 *raftans*. The *tellys* has 16 *muds*. Of the *mud* there are two kinds, the *mud el shoone* (or the granary mud), and the *mud el soogy* (or souky), the market mud; 16 of the mud el shoone make 9 mud el soogy. The seed of the 14 feddáns of durra was 3½ mud soogy. The produce yielded 40 muds for each associate, or 1040 for the whole, which makes 297 for each mud of seed. The durra is usually reckoned at 300 for 1 of seed. The corn produce at Esne in middling years 25 from 1; in the better ground of the neighbouring plains of Thebes, it produces 35 for 1.

The present system of government is to oblige
the peasants to sow the whole ground belonging to
their village, whether good or bad, whether elevated
or not, and therefore, whether irrigable or not.
The bad ground is then partitioned out amongst the
cultivators, and they must pay the taxes from it in
the same proportion as from the good. Of late all
the peasants' cattle has likewise been taxed, and
they are to pay the tithes from it, a thing never
before known in Egypt, and I believe, unknown in
any other part of the Turkish dominions. The grain
which they do not want for their own families,
they are not at liberty to sell at pleasure, but
must let government have it at a fixed price. The
erdeb of durra was then worth at Esne 5¾ piasters
1 Spanish dollar = 8 piasters; 1 piaster = 40 paras.

472.

فم يسبح و يد تذبح.

A mouth that prays, a hand that kills.

On hypocrites.

473.

في الزوايا خبايا

In the corners are hidden treasures.

Wealth is sometimes found where least expected.
زوايا plural of زاوية "the corner of a building." خبايا
"hidden treasures," a word of frequent use.

474.

فرَّ من المطر قعد تحت المزرآب

He fled from the rain, and sat down under the water-spout.

475.

فرد كلمة تكفي العاقل

One single word only is sufficient for the wise.

فرد instead of واحد is much used in the Syrian dialect; not so frequently in the Egyptian.

476.*

في كل راس حكمة

In every head is some wisdom.

477.

في بردعته مسلّة

In his jackass-saddle sticks a needle.

Secret vexations plague him. بردعة the saddle for asses used in Egypt. مسلّة a long iron packing needle, used likewise in sewing the saddle.

478.

فريخ البطّ عوّام

The young ones of the duck are swimmers.

Young minds are inflamed by example. عوم or يعوم in the common Egyptian dialect, signifies "to swim." يسبح is likewise used, but not frequently.

479.

في الطَّبَقَة الوسطانية يبعبص الفوقانيين و يضرط علي التحتانيين

(*Standing*) *in the middle window, he tickles the
    hinder parts of those who sit in the upper
    window, and insults (by offensive noises) those in
    the lower window.*

He behaves with vulgarity and indecency to
people above and below him. طبقه among many
significations means "a window." يبعبص in the
Egyptian dialect, "to tickle the hinder parts of a
person;" it has also another sense.

480.

فلان حجّ قال و من نكحسه يتجاور

*Such a man performed the pilgrimage. " Yes,"
    quoth one, "and for his bad doings remains
    resident at Mekka."*

يتجاور to become a neighbour either of the
Beitullah of Mekka, or of the Mosque of Medina,
or any other celebrated mosque; or to reside there
for some time, which is regarded as very meritorious.
Those persons, especially foreigners, who attend
lectures in a mosque, are for that reason called
مجاورين Thus at Cairo the neighbours of the *Azhar*
(مجاورين الزهر) are far famed.

481.*

نقر و حماقة ما يتفق

Poverty and anger do not agree.

The poor must have pliant tempers. حماقة in

Egypt means "anger;" it is sometimes used, but not often, for "folly."

482.

نوطه بحواشي و ما تحتها شي

A napkin with (fine) borders and nothing under it.

Puff without reality. Presents to people of high rank are often placed upon a board or plate, and covered with fine embroidered towels or handkerchiefs (نوطه).

483.

فقرا و يمشوا مشي المرا

They are paupers, and walk about with the air of grandees.

484.

فرحنا بالنيل جا النيل غرقنا

We rejoiced at (the rising of) the Nile; the Nile came and we were drowned.

485.

في راسه صوت لا بد ما يرعقه

He has a voice in his head, and will certainly give it utterance.

A person follows his inclination or natural propensities. The saying is originally applied to a jackass that brays notwithstanding the severest beating.

486.

في كل يوم يزداد ابن ادم عقل جديد

Every day man increases in new understanding.

487.

فَرغ العُرس بمرقه و لبس كل واحد خلقه

*The wedding with its broth (i.e. the entertainments)
concluded; and then every one put on his rags.*

When disguise is no longer necessary or advan-
tageous the natural character is resumed. At
weddings even the poorest people dress, if not in
their own, at least in fine clothes borrowed for the
occasion. خلق "a torn cloth," "a rag."

488.

فار وقع من السقف قال له القط بسم الله قال ابعد انت عني

*A mouse fell from the roof. "Come, take some
refreshment," said the cat. "Stand thou off,"
she replied.*

Mistrust any offer of assistance from the enemy.
بسم الله is used as an invitation to partake of food,
&c. To decline it the reply is هنيًا "May it be
wholesome food to thee!" ابعد عني a common
expression implying with harshness "keep off,"
"stand off."

489.

افسد من الأَرَضة

(He is) of more corrupt doings than the moth.

الأَرَضة is the moth that feeds upon clothes, books,
furniture, &c.

490.

في كفّه رقّ ابليس مفتاح

The enchantments of the devil are (only) a key in his hand.

رقّ plural of رقية "a charm," "enchantment."
The saying is addressed to a malicious sorcerer.
The dealing in charms and incantations is extremely
common throughout Egypt. There is not any
village, however small, in which they may not be
obtained from the *fakyh,* or village priest.

491.*

فرّ من الموت و في الموت وقع

He fled from death, and fell into it.

492.*

فرّ اخزاه الله خيرٌ من قتل يرحمه الله

" He fled, disgrace upon him!" is better than, " He was slain, God have mercy upon him!"

Said in derision of cowardly soldiers. The
expression اخزاك الله or, as they likewise say in
Egypt الله يخزيك is very common.

493.

فوق كل طامة طامة

Upon every misfortune another misfortune.

One misfortune after another.

494.

الفضل للمبتدي و ان احسن المقتبدي

The merit belongs to the beginner, should even the
successor do better.

To the same purport is a phrase often used
الفضل للمتقدم "the merit belongs to the predecessor."
This is taken from the subjoined beautiful verses,
celebrated among the Arabs, and inserted by *Harîrî*
into the Introduction of his Makamát, assigning
thereby the merit for that species of poetry to his
predecessor *Hamadáni,* surnamed *Bedȳa e Zamán.*
They have been ascribed to several poets, but were
probably composed by *Ibn Malek Ibn e'Rakaa,* of
Damascus, who lived in the eighth century of the
Christian era.

فلو قبل مبكاها بكيت صبابة
بسعدي شفيت القلب قبل التندّم
ولكن بكت قبلي فهيّج لي البكا
بكاها فقلت الفضل للمتقدم

If before she herself wept, love for Sada had caused
   my tears to flow,
I should have lightened my heart before repentance
   (choked it);
But she wept first, her tears excited mine,
The merit, I cried, belongs to the predecessor.

حرف القاف

495.

قَحبة مستورة و لا حُرّة مبهرجة

A decent public woman, rather than an indecent
honest woman.

مستور "decently covered," "decent in circumstances;" it is applied both to the character and
condition of a person. مبهرج or مبهرجة is a woman
who frequently lifts up a corner of her veil so that
people may catch a glimpse of her face or her fine
jewels, or else one who stretches out her legs to
display her ankle-rings, and in general behaves with
as much indecency as she can without quite exposing
her character.

قَحبة is a generic term applied in Egypt to all
sorts of bad and public women. There is a particular
class of the latter in this country, respecting whom
some notices may prove interesting. In every town,
indeed it may be said in almost every large village,
of Egypt, individuals are found belonging to a tribe
of prostitutes called *Ghazýe* (غزية or in the plural
Ghowázy غوازي). They are a race distinct from all
other public women, and relate with pride that their
origin is Arabian, and that they are of the true

Bedouin blood. Among themselves they assume the name of *Barameke* or *Barmeky* (برامكة), by which, however, they are less generally known than by that of *Ghowázy*. They boast that their origin is derived from the celebrated *Barmeky* (or Barmecide) family, the viziers of Haroun er' Rasheed; but in what manner any descent can be traced to them, why they emigrated to Egypt, and how they chose to adopt their vile profession, not one of them knows. They usually marry among themselves, at least the males never marry any girl but a Barmeky; and few of the Barmeky females condescend to take a husband of any other tribe. All their females, without exception, are educated for the purpose of prostitution. Their law is, that a girl, as soon as she is marriageable, *must* yield to the embraces of a stranger, and soon after be married to a young man of her own tribe. Thus the husband is never permitted to receive his bride in a state of virgin purity; but the Ghowázy father sells the first favours of his daughter to a stranger, making a bargain with the highest bidder, generally in pre-sence of the sheikh of the village, or chief of the town, in which the parties reside. These women, and all the females of this tribe marry, immediately after the nuptial ceremony, receive the visits of any man who presents himself, while the husband performs the duties of a menial servant in the family; he is also the musician who plays when his wife dances in public, and is consequently employed in seeking for persons who may be induced to visit his wife, with whom he himself cohabits only by stealth; for a Ghazye would think herself disgraced, or at least would be exposed to the sneers of the sisterhood, if it were known that she admitted her husband to any familiarity or participation in the enjoyment of her charms. Among them, I have reason to believe, (but am not certain,) that the Ghazy (so the male is called) has but one wife. The men never follow any profession; they are neither cultivators, nor traders, nor artists; the dealing in asses, of which they rear an excellent breed, being the only branch of industry to which they apply themselves, besides the sale of their partners' charms. They are as much despised as their females are distinguished and often honoured; the birth of a male child is considered by a Ghazye as a great misfortune, because he is an unprofitable article—a mere incumbrance—and the whole male sex look up to the females for food, clothes, and protection. The Ghowázys have in every town or considerable village a small quarter assigned to them, where they live in large huts or tents, seldom in houses; never associating with other public women, whom they regard as much inferior to themselves in rank. They are generally, but not always, dancers and singers, and as such many travellers have seen and admired them. Like true Bedouins they are constantly moving about, either paying visits to the sisterhood established in neighbouring places, attending the country fairs, or the camps of the troops. They have made it a law among them, never to refuse the embraces of any person, whatever may be his condition, so that he pays : at country fairs, therefore, the most fashionable Ghazye, glittering with gold, will admit the visit of any clown or fellah for a sum not exceeding twopence. Some of them have accumulated considerable wealth and keep great establishments. Half-a-dozen black female slaves, (the profits of whose prostitution they claim as their own property,) two or three dromedaries, as many horses, half-a-dozen asses, are not unfrequently seen in one family; while the dress and ornaments of those females, consisting in gold-embroidered silk gowns, and many chains of sequins that hang about the head, neck, and breast, with heavy golden bracelets, are sometimes worth from two to three hundred pounds sterling. In features they may be distinguished from the common Egyptians, and appear to bear traces of Arabian origin, especially in their fine aquiline noses. Their beauty is famous throughout Egypt ; the greater number, however, cannot be reckoned handsome, yet I have seen some that might have served as models of Phryne for a painter; their skin not being browner than that of the inhabitants of southern Europe. Instances are not uncommon of a Ghazye marrying a village sheikh, especially of the Howara Arabs settled in Upper Egypt, who consider it an honour to carry off so fair a prize, nor would the Ghazye bestow herself in matrimony on any common peasant. But these instances only occur when the Ghazye has lost her husband, or divorced him, and has become tired of her mode of life, in the outset of which she can never be induced to renounce her hereditary profession. When such an event is to take place, the Ghazye, before she marries the sheikh, makes a solemn vow upon the tomb of some saint never to be unfaithful to her new husband, and sacrifices a sheep in honour of that patron. I have been assured on good authority that no Ghazye married under these circumstances was ever known to violate her vow. The number in Egypt is very considerable ; I believe that they may be fairly estimated, males and females, at from six to eight thousand persons. Their principal settlements are in the towns of the Delta, and in Upper Egypt at Kenne, where they have a colony of at least three hundred individuals. On the great festival of the Saint el Bedowy, at Tanta in the Delta, (which is celebrated three times every year,) an hundred thousand persons sometimes crowd together from all parts of Egypt, to perform a pilgrimage resembling in many respects that of Mekka, which swallows up the savings collected by the poorer classes of Cairo. At one of those festivals I have seen above six hundred Ghazye assembled in tents pitched about the town. Some of the most wealthy Ghazye perform the pilgrimage to Mekka themselves in great state, and assume ever after the honourable title of Hadjy, not changing however their mode of life. The Ghowázys are protected by the government of Egypt, to which they pay an annual capitation tax. In the time of the Mamelouks their influence in the open country was very considerable,

and the protection of a Ghazye was courted by
many respectable persons. The Arnaut soldiers,
who are at present masters of Egypt, have plundered
several and killed others in fits of jealousy, so that
many have fled from the garrison towns into the
open country. They have a custom in Upper Egypt,
on the feast-day after Ramadhan, of paying visits to
all the first people of the town or village, when they
dance for a few minutes in the court-yard of the
house and receive a present at parting. Their
behaviour towards those who do not meddle with
them is much less indecent than might be imagined;
but woe to him whose affections they captivate!
At every place where they are numerous one of
them is regarded as head of their community, and
assumes the title of "Emeer el Nezel" (امير النزل),
or "chief of the settlement;" which, however, does
not invest her with any authority over the others.
At Cairo itself their number is but small; they live
all together in a large khan, called *Hosh Bardak*,
just below the castle. In a city where among
women of every rank chastity is so scarce as at
Cairo, it could not be expected that public prostitution should thrive.

The Ghowázys have established among themselves
a vocabulary of the most common nouns and phrases,
in which they are able to converse without being
understood by those who visit them.

There is another tribe of public women in Egypt
called *Halebye* (حلبيّة), they are fewer in numbers
than the *Ghowázys*, but like them intermarry among

themselves. The men are tinkers, and horse or ass
doctors; the women for the greater part, but I
believe not all, common prostitutes. They wander
over the country much like Gypsies. Of the latter,
which are called here غاجر *Ghadjar* (in Syria
Korbat), very few families are found in Egypt; they
are more numerous in Syria.

496.

قيمة كل انسان ما يحسنه

The value of each man consists in what he does well.

يحسن is here equivalent to يفعل الحسن مع It
is in this sense usually, but not always, applied to
handiwork. The Syrians say ما بيحسن for ما يحسن
meaning "I cannot (do it)," which the Egyptians
express by ما يقدر

497.*

قحبة ما كنست بيتها كنست المساجد قال دي قحبة
تحب الثواب

*A harlot did not sweep her own house, but cleaned
out the mosque. A certain person said, "that
harlot loves goodly works."*

498.

القحبة ما تتوب و الماء في الزير ما يروب

*A harlot does not repent; and water in a jar does
not become sour milk.*

زير a large jar in which the water is kept for

every family's use. يروب is applied to milk when it
turns sour.   In Egypt, therefore, sour milk is called
رائب

499.

قمر و زيت دا خراب بيت

Moonshine and oil, those are the ruin of a house.

To light the lamp while the moon shines is an
extravagant expense that will ruin the family. قمر
is often used instead of نور القمر

500.

قرد يحرس ترمس قال انظر الحارس و المارس

A monkey watches (a field of) tormus. "Look," said
one, " at the guard and the crop."

This alludes to a despicable person occupying a
despicable office. المارس in the dialect of the peasants frequently is used instead of الزرع "the sown
field." *Tormus* is the *lupinus*, a bean of bitter taste
and but little esteemed. A person to whom a small
compliment is given, shows his contempt of the gift
by returning it and saying to the donor قزقز به ترمس
"(buy and) chew some tormus with it."

Boiled *tormus* beans are sold in the morning at
the bázár, and principally eaten by children without
either salt or butter. The meal of this bean is used
instead of soap by the poorer classes for washing
their hands, and on this account it is very generally
cultivated in Egypt.

501.

قالوا للعميان الزيت غلي قالوا دا شي مستغنيين عنه

They said to some blind men, "oil is become dear."
They replied, "that is a thing with which we can
dispense."

استغني means here (as observed in the explanation
of Proverb 259) "not to be in want of." دا used
instead of هذا

502.

قالوا الحمير الجباسة يوم القيامة يوم عظيم قالوا ما لبسنا
برادع و لا اكلنا شعير

They said to the asses of the gypsum mill, "the day
of resurrection is a terrible day!" "We have
neither worn saddles nor eaten barley," they
replied.

Those have most to dread punishment in the
other world who lead a life of undeserved enjoyment
in this. The idle asses kept merely for pleasure in
Cairo have fine saddles, and are fed with plenty of
barley or beans; while the hard-working ass goes
with a bare back, and gets nothing to eat but straw.
عظيم "great, wonderful, terrible." The gypsum or
plaster used at Cairo is brought from the eastern
mountain opposite to Heloüan, a village on the bank
of the Nile, about five hours distant to the south of
Cairo. The whole desert is overspread in those
mountains with loose gypsum, covered with a thin
coat of sand. The gypsum is pulverised in the mills
at Cairo.

503.

قال السمك البنّي ان لقيت احسن مَني ما تاكلني

The fish binny said, "if thou canst find a better fish than myself do not eat me."

The *binny* is reckoned the finest tasted fish of the river Nile. This proverb is applied to fools whose vanity is such that they pride themselves on the circumstance which contributes to their mis-fortune, because it distinguishes them among their equals.

504.

قرعة و تضارب علي المشط

He is scabby-headed and quarrels about the comb.

On a person's disputing about a thing of which he does not stand in need.

505.

قراطيس علي قوم مفاليس

(Like) assignments upon paupers.

تمسكات or جمّ used instead of اوراق or قراطيس or بوالس " titles, receipts, assignments, bills," &c.

506.*

قفل علي خرابة

A lock on a ruined place.

Said of unnecessary pains taken to preserve what is not worth keeping.

507.

قالت المغاربة لاهل مصر ليش ما تحبّونا قالوا من الخلاق
الرديّة

*The Moggrebyns said to the people of Cairo, "Why
do not ye love us?" "On account of your ill-
natured character," they replied.*

This saying is applied to a person who expresses
his surprise at not having any friends. The Moggrebyns form a colony of very wealthy merchants at
Cairo, established in the quarters of Ghoorye and
Fahamyn, who trade in the produce of their native
country. They have the reputation of being ill-bred,
surly, proud, and very obstinate, and are therefore
disliked ; although, with respect to probity, they
bear a character superior to the Moslims of any other
nation. The word of a Moggrebyn (مغربية كلمة) has
become a proverbial saying in trade, but nobody
ever mentions the word of a Syrian, a Hedjázi, or a
Turk.

508.

قالوا يا قسيس يردّك الله شمّاس قال دي درجة لاسفل

*They said, "O priest! may God make you a lay
brother once more!" "That is a step downwards," he replied.*

On foolish congratulations or wishes. In saying
الله يردّك a compliment is intended, meaning "God
restore thee to thy prosperous state!" Thus they
say العافية يردّك الله or شاب يردّك الله "God restore
thee to health!" "God restore thee to youth!"

509.

قالوا ايش حال مريضكم قالوا بخير كان يبتق علي
الارض صار يبصق علي صدره

*They asked, "How does your patient?" "Very
well," they replied, "he used to spit upon the
ground, now he spits upon his breast."*

On the delusive consolations offered by medical
attendants. A patient who cannot even throw his
spittle upon the ground, must be, of course, in a
state of extreme debility.

510.

قالوا للدجاجة كلي و لا تبعنزي قالت ما اقدر اخلّي
عادتي

*They said to the hen, "Eat, and do not scatter (the
corn) about." "I cannot leave off my habits," she
replied.*

It is useless to instruct an inveterate scoundrel
in morals. يبعنز among the Egyptians means "to
throw about," "to scatter;" it comes from the
word بعنزة but differs in signification.

511.

قرموط ملتوت سدر في بركة صابون

*(Like) a karmoot rubbed with seder in a tank of soap
(water).*

This is said of a person whom it is difficult to
catch or find; one who eludes all search. قرموط *kar-*

moot is a fish of the river Nile, without any scales, and of a very smooth skin. *Seder* (سدر) signifies the leaves of the *nebek* or *seder* tree, (rhamnus lotus,) which, being dried and pulverized, are used as soap by people of the poorest class in washing their hands, and by the richer classes in washing the dead bodies of their friends. ملتوت in the Egyptian dialect has the same sense as مدهون

512.*

قال ايش مراد الاعمي قال قفة قرون ان لم ينظر يناطح

It was asked, " What is the wish of the blind?"
" A basket full of horns," they replied, " if he does not see he may like butting."

The blind men of Cairo, especially those quartered in the mosques, are notorious for their very quarrelsome temper. The multitudes of blind men daily fed in the Mosque el Azhar have frequently committed violent outrages in fighting one with another.

513.

قالوا للديك ايش ابصرت في نومك قال يغربلوا

They asked the cock, " What hast thou seen in thy sleep?" " I saw people sifting (corn)," he replied.

514.*

قال يا ابي !الذي يغسل يده ياكل معنا قال و لا انت ايضا

*"Father," he said, "the person who washes his hand
is he to eat with us?" "Neither he nor thou
also," he replied.*

On a person who, confident of obtaining some
advantage for himself, endeavours to thwart others
in their wishes, but finds at last that his own
prospects have vanished. In the East, before a man
begins to dine he always washes his hands, or at
least the right hand, which alone is used at meals.

515.

قالوا للغار خذلك رطلين سكر و وصل دي الكتاب للقط
قال الاجرة طيبة لكن فيها مشقة

*They said to the mouse, "Take these two pounds of
sugar and carry this letter to the cat." "The
fee is good enough," she replied, "but (the
business) is tiresome."*

كتاب often used in Egypt for مكتوب "a letter."

516.

قالوا للحمار ليش ما تشتر قال ما ينطلي علّي المحال
*They asked the ass, "Why do not you ruminate?"
"Conceit," he said, "never deludes me."*

الاشترار "the chewing and ruminating of cows
and camels." ما ينطلي علي المحال verbatim, "deceit

cannot be gilt (or laid like gold leaf) over or upon
me," "does not make me appear to myself better
than I am." The expression هذا ما ينطلي عني is
often used, and conveys the same meaning as "this
can never enter my head," "I can have no idea of
it," "I am not to be gilt over with this."

517.

قطع الفار بالزيت الحار ما هو كثير

*To cut off the mice with hemp oil, is not too much
expense.*

Do not care for expense in freeing yourself from
an enemy. The hemp oil mixed with arsenic is used
as poison for mice.

518.

قال يا عبد اشتريتك قال هذا لك قال تهرب قال هذا لي

*He said, "O slave, I have bought thee." "That is
thy business," he replied. "Wilt thou run away?"
"That is my business," he answered.*

519.

قطعوها صاحت للطنبورة

*They cut it to pieces; it served well for (the covering
of) the drum.*

Commonly said of a broken or spoiled piece of
any thing, which can, however, be still employed in
some manner, so as not to be wholly useless.

520.

قالوا للديب ما لك ورا هذة الغنيمات قال ترابهم ينفع
للعوينات

*They said to the wolf, " For what art thou following
those poor little sheep?" He replied, " The dust
(upon which they tread) is good for poor little
eyes."*

On the hypocritical professions of tyrants. The
diminutive is often used not only because the object
in question is really smaller or inferior in quantity
or quality, but to give a kind of *bonhomie* to the
expression ; and in this sense the Bedouins especially
use it on many occasions. Thus "poor little thing"
might be applied in a kind and compassionate
manner to a person by no means diminutive in
stature or wanting money. عوينات is the diminutive
or تصغير of عيون the eyes. ما لك is a common
expression in Egypt, not implying "what is it *to*
thee ?" but, "what is the matter *with* thee ?"
"what dost thou want?" The Syrians say in the
same sense ايش بك

521.

قالوا للبقر اذا متم ما يكفنوكم قالوا ليتهم يخلّوا جلودنا
علينا

*They asked the cows, "If you die, do they not put
you into shrouds?" They replied, "Would to
God they may leave our skins upon us!"*

Instead of ليت the Egyptians more frequently
say ريت, and then it would stand ريتهم يخلّوا

522.

قال يا سيدي نحات قال يا راجل سيدك ياكله بقشره

"*My Lord,*" *he said,* "*(I beg of you) the melon peels.*"
"*Man,*" *quoth he,* "*thy Lord eats the melon
together with the melon peels.*"

نحات signifies a piece of melon peel. When a
person eats melons in the bázár or before the coffee
shops, he is always accosted by beggars, who ask for
the peels, which they eat, as all the peasants do
when hungry.

523.

قرد ضاف عفريت قالوا له ماجردة يا ابن الشيخ

A monkey solicited hospitality from demons. "*Young
gentleman,*" *they replied,* "*the house is quite
empty of provisions.*"

It is in vain to ask charity from wretches. ضاف
in the Egyptian dialect is the same as طَلَب الضيافة
in opposition to يصيف which signifies "to grant
hospitality." ابن الشيخ is a title given from mere
politeness and equivalent to "gentleman," or
"young gentleman." ماجردة is to be understood as
if preceded by الدار "the house from which every
thing has been removed," or "which has remained
empty of provisions."

524.

قد ضلّ مَن كانت العميان تهديه

Verily he loses his way whom blind men guide.

A verse is cited which expresses the same meaning :—

اذا كان الغراب دليل قومٍ
يمروا بهم علي جيف الكلاب

When crows are the guides of people,
They lead them to the carcases of dogs.

525.

قد تَبْلي المليحة بالطلاق

Even the handsome (woman) experiences the mis-
fortune of divorce.

This is said in consolation of people's sufferings.

526.*

قد يتوقّي السيف و هو مغمد

Truly, the sword inspires dread even in its scabbard.

527.*

قلمه لا يرعف الّا بالشرّ

From his pen nothing flows but malice.

يرعف originally means "blood flowing out of the nose." The reproach conveyed in this proverb is more applicable to Western than to Eastern writers.

Oriental authors are distinguished for great gentleness towards each other; paper wars seldom rage among them, and they render justice one to another perhaps in a strain of excessive panegyric; and if they correct an error, it is with coolness and moderation. The total want of publications resembling our Reviews, and the fear of broaching new doctrines or opinions, contribute probably to this spirit of indulgence.

528.

القصاب لا تهوله كثرة الغنم

The butcher is not startled at the multiplicity of sheep.

A tyrant perpetrates bloody acts without compunction. يهول "to be afraid," or "amazed."

529.*

قبل السحاب أصابني الوكف

Before the clouds (appeared) the rain came upon me.

The accident happened quite unexpectedly. The term وكف for "rain," is no longer used at Cairo.

530.

اقبح من قول بلا فعل

(It is still) worse than a promise without performance.

قول a word, a saying, a promise.

حرف الكاف

531.

كَبِّب و الله المسبِّب

Be diligent, and God will send profit.

يكبِّب "to make small balls or pills;" this
generally implies "to be diligently occupied," "to
work carefully." المسبِّب الله "God is the first cause,
the cause of causes." This is often said in trade,
and then means, "God is the cause of thy goods
being sold, the cause of thy profits" (جعله اسباب).
The word اسباب in the Egyptian dialect, signifies
"trade, buying and selling in general." يتسبِّب "he
trades." رجل متسبِّب for "trader or merchant," is
more commonly used than رجل تاجر

532.

كانها من سواقي الجِيزة وقعت اضراسها و قتلت ماية شب

*As if she was one of the water-wheels of Djyze, her
back teeth fell out, and one hundred oxen were
killed by her (with the work).*

This saying is used in derision of old women.
سواقي plural of ساقية a water-wheel. ضرس means the

back teeth of a person, also the teeth of a water-wheel. شب is the Egyptian pronunciation of ساب "a young man;" the peasants also give this name to a strong ox—hence the pun which occurs in this place. If a water-wheel be half broken, the oxen that draw it are soon overworked and killed by excessive labour. The people of Djyze are the Bæotians of Egypt, they are despised for their stupidity and slovenly negligence, and often afford subject for ridicule.

533.

كل ما تشتهيه نفسك و البس ما تلبس الناس

Eat whatever thou likest, but dress as others do.

Do whatever you like at home, but in public behave according to received usage.

534.

كلب ينبح ما يعض

A dog that barks does not bite.

535.*

كم خروف عند الشوا و كم كلب في المراح

How many sheep at the roaster's? and how many dogs in the sheepfold?

How many good people are sacrificed while the wicked enjoy their life in repose. الشوا the person who sells roasted meat in the bázár.

536.

كفّ معوّد بالاخذ بعيد ما يعطي

A hand accustomed to take is far from giving.

بعيد انه يعطي is here put for بعيد ما يعطي

537.

كلاب الصيد وجوههم مَخْربشة

The hunting dogs have scratched faces.

The face of a milksop does not show any marks
of labour or fatigue. مَخْربش in the Egyptian dialect
"scratched."

538.

كيف ما ضرِبت الاقرع يسيل دمه

*In whatever manner thou strikest a scabby-headed
person (on the head), his blood will flow.*

A man is easily wounded in his weak part.

539.

كان سندال فصار مطرقة

*He was an iron block or anvil, and then become a
hammer.*

The same meaning is also expressed by the
phrase

مضروب اليوم ضارب

Beaten—but to-day beater

540.

كسل ما يطعم عسل

The lazy is not fed on honey.

541.

كل من خبز الرعفة و لا تاكل من خبز المنانة

*Eat of the bread made by a woman with a bleeding
nose; but do not eat the bread of her who constantly reminds thee of having given it.*

The dirtiest bread, made by a رعفة "a woman
with a bleeding nose." المنان signifies a person who
recounts his own good works, and reminds another
of the favours he has conferred on him. In the
East, there is no sort of insulting language which
hurts the feelings so much as being reminded of
favours conferred; probably because the people are
conscious of their own ingratitude.

542.

كل راس مطاطية تحتها الف بلية

*Under every down-hanging head dwell a thousand
mischiefs.*

This is said of persons who in company sit with
downcast eyes and low-bent head, brooding all the
while on evil designs. مطاطي in the Egyptian dialect signifies " bent downwards."

543.*

كل من قال نار احترق فمه

Whoever cries " Fire," has he his mouth burnt?

Those who cry out most loudly have often the least reason to complain.

544.

كشكار دايم و لا علامة مقطوعة

Coarse meal for ever, rather than fine flour at
certain times only.

This proverb is founded upon the saying of Mohammed recorded in the Hadyth or Traditions :

خير العمال ادومها و انقل

The best works are those which last, although they
should not be of great importance.

كشكار is the " coarse meal used by peasants." علامة " the flour of meal." مقطوعة " cut off," " at intervals only."

545.

كل شاة معلّقة من عرقوبها

Every sheep is suspended by its (own) heels.

In a future state, none will be made to suffer for the crimes of others. عرقوب is the sinew or tendon (of Achilles) by which butchers hang up the slaughtered sheep.

546.

كفّي عني فساكي ما اريد بخورك

*Let me only be excused from thy bad smells; I do
not want thy perfumes.*

A speech in the closet from a husband to his
wife. Leave off thy rudeness, I require no civilities.

547.

كل ما ضربت له وتد علّق مخلاة

*As often as I strike a woted for him he hangs up
(another) barley-sack.*

No sooner is one business finished than he sets
about another. Among Arab sheiks in the desert,
as well as in the villages, it is customary that when
guests arrive on horseback, each horse is attached by
a chain on his legs to an iron spike driven for that
purpose into the ground, either before the tent or in
the court-yard of the house. This spike, about eight
inches long, is called *woted* (وتد) and every horseman
carries one with him. As soon as the guest alights
from his horse the master of the tent or house takes
from him the barley-sack (مخلاة) in which the horse
receives his food, (and which the horseman likewise
carries with him,) and hangs it upon a post or nail.
From this his people take it in the evening and fill
it with barley. In this proverb the master's servant
complains, that as soon as he has driven one *woted*
into the ground, another horseman arrives, whose
barley-sack is hung up, and whose *woted* must likewise be driven into the ground.

548.*

كونوا اخوة و اتحاسبوا حساب التجار

*Be brothers, and keep between you the accounts of
merchants.*

549.

كف جاه و لا ويبة مال

*A handful of consideration rather than a woebe of
riches.*

Woebe (ويبة) is an Egyptian corn measure, of
which six make an *erdeb.*

550.

كان يحلف بقطع يمينة صار يحلف بزكاة ماله

*He was wont to swear " by the cutting off of his right
hand !"   He now swears "by the giving of his
money to the poor !"*

This is said of persons who having been poor
acquire wealth and immediately assume the language
of rich people. A low fellow without money, swears,
" May my hand be cut off if—" (the amputation of
the hand is a thief's punishment). The great and
rich men swear, " I will give my whole estates or
wealth to the poor if—."

551.

كل و اشرب و خلّي الدنيا تخرب

Eat and drink, and let the world go to ruin.

552.

كل واحد في سوقه يبيع خروقه

Every one sells his rags in his own market.

Every one parades or displays his distinguishing qualities in his own circle of acquaintances.

553.

كرامة لقصرك نهدّ خصّنا

For the sake of thy palace shall we demolish our hut?

الخصّ is an Arab hut constructed of brushwood or reeds. قصر a stately building or palace. From its plural القصر which the peasants pronounce *el oksor*, we have formed Luxor, the temple of Thebes. كرامة ي (pronounced *kormály*) does not mean in the usual sense "for my honour," or "to my honour," but merely "for my sake."

554.

كريم ما يستغني

The generous is never satisfied with riches.

He wants money that he may bestow it on others.

555.

كلنا بهذه العلّة و الطبيب الله

We are all (afflicted) with this disease; God is the physician.

Said in offering consolation to others.

556.

كل الهدية و اكسر الزبدية

Eat the present (sent to thee) and break the dish (in which it was brought).

The dish will otherwise remind you of the obligation. زبدية; is a small basin of earthenware glazed on the inside; it is usual to serve up sweetmeats in dishes of this kind.

557.

كل ممنوع حلو

Every thing forbidden is sweet.

558.

كل انسان وهمّه

Every man—and his own care.

Every person has his share of trouble. وهمّة put instead of بهمّه

559.

كن يهودي تام و الّا فلا تلعب بالتوراة

Be a thorough Jew, or else do not play with the Old Testament.

Be sincerely attached to a religion however bad, rather than laugh at this, thy religion. التوراة the Books of Moses, which are respected by the Moslims as derived from heaven, but which they believe to have suffered by the interpolations of Jews and Christians, because the mission of Mohammed was, as they pretend, foretold in the original text.

560.*

كِهرّة تاكل ٠ اولادها

Like a cat that eats her own young ones.

Said of a mother who neglects her children.

561.*

كلام الليل يمحوه النهار

The day obliterates the word (or promise) of the night.

This verse was quoted in reply to Haroun el Rasheed by a beautiful woman who at night had promised that she would bestow her favours on him the next morning ; but when day appeared she declined the performance of her promise. It has thus become proverbial. A similar saying is more generally current at Cairo, expressing that "*the promise of the night is rubbed with butter, which melts away when the day shines upon it.*"

كلام الليل مدهون بزبدة يطلع عليه النهار و يسيح

This means, that, when passion has ceased, we forget the promise made while it influenced us.

562.

كدنب الحمار لا يزيد و لا ينقص

Like the ass's tail, it never increases, and never diminishes.

Applied to one who remains constantly in the same condition. There is a popular notion, I know not whether founded on fact, that the tail of an ass never increases in length, but remains as it was when the animal was born, except as to the growth of hair.   ذنب is used in Egypt for دنب

563.

كالابرة تكسي الناس و هي عريانة

Like a needle that clothes people and is itself naked.

This alludes to persons under similar circumstances ; and is taken from that fine verse—

كست قيصرًا ثوب التجمال و تبعًا

وكسري و باتت وهي عارية التجسم

The same meaning is still more forcibly expressed in the following verse—

صِرتُ كاتّي ذُبالةً نَصبت تضي للناس وهي تُحرق

I have become like a wick placed in a lamp,
It affords light to the people while itself is burnt.

564.*

كن ذكورٌ اذا كنت كذوبًا

Be of good mémory if you become a liar.

565.*

كالكماة لا اصل ثابت و لا فرع نابت

Like the truffle, without any (known) origin, and not sending forth any branches.

كماة is a species of truffle found in the deserts

of Syria, (I believe not in Egypt,) which affords
nourishment to many Bedouin families. Like the
European truffles they produce no plant, nor is it
known how they are propagated. The Arabs say
that they are produced by thunder and lightning.

566.

كلام لَين و ظلم بَين

Soft words, but open injustice.

567.*

كم من يد ضعافا الكسب خرقا في الانفاق

*How many a hand weak in gaining is prodigal in
spending.*

568.

الكلب ما ينبح في داره

The dog does not bark in his own house.

569.*

كل عبد ان جاع سرق و ان شبع فسق

*Every slave when he is hungry steals, and when he is
satiated, practises wickedness.*

On the effects of poverty and wealth upon low-
minded persons.

570.

كالعنين يفتخر بزب ابيه

Like the impotent, who glories in the vigour of his
father.

Applied to those who without any just personal
pretensions assume airs in consequence of the merits
of their ancestors. عنين signifies one naturally impotent. The ancient Arabs quoted on this subject
the following fine verse—

ان الفتي مَن يقول ها انا ذا
ليس الفتي من يقول كان ابي

He is the truly noble youth, who says " Behold, I am
the man," not he who says " My father was."

What is above translated *vigour*, is in the
original Arabic a term for which the Dictionary may
be consulted.

حرف الام

571.

ليس التخبر كالعيان

Hearsay is not like ocular testimony.

مشاهدة العيون is ocular evidence, equivalent to عيان

572.

لو ابصرت بختي دسته بالقدم

If thou wert to see my luck, thou wouldst trample it under foot.

Said by the unlucky.

573.

ليت الفتجل يهضم نفسه

Did but the radish digest its ownself!

Could we but rid ourselves of the person whom we have invited to be our assistant. It is commonly believed in the East that radishes eaten at or after meals facilitate the digestion of other food, although they themselves remain undigested in the stomach.

574.

لو فتش ابن ادم علي التخبز ما اكله

If a man were to inquire after (the dirty manner of making) bread, he would not eat it.

575.

لو يكون الفلاح من ذهب لكان بيضه من خشب

If the fellah were made of gold, certain parts of him would be of wood.

Although a low person may attain an exalted station, and however his manners may be improved, some remnants of his former meanness will always

be conspicuous. Here may be quoted the following
verse—

لقد كشف الاثرأ منك خلايقاً من اللوم كانت في غطآ
من الفقرِ

*Riches have disclosed in thy character the bad
qualities formerly concealed by thy poverty.*

576.

لو اوقدت لك العشرة ما رايتهم آلا ظلام

*If I had lighted for thee the ten (fingers as candles)
thou wouldst still regard them as if they were in
darkness.*

Said of one who forgets or never acknowledges
the most signal services rendered to him.

577.

لو لا الكسورة ما كانت الفاخورة

Were it not for fractures there would be no pottery.

Misfortunes are not without some good consequences. كسورة in the Egyptian dialect for كسر

578.

لو ان رزقه في است الكلب اكله

*If his gain lay in the hinder (or filthiest) part of a
dog he would eat it.*

On a person descending to the vilest modes of
obtaining profit.

579.

لو لا شالوني من تحته كنت قتلته

If they had not dragged me from under him, I should have killed him.

Said in ridicule of a bragging fellow.

580.

لو سكت فمه تكلمت استه

If his mouth were silent another part of him would speak.

Alluding to one who talked incessantly.

581.*

لو كان في الحداية خير ما فاتت الصيادين

If the falcon had been good for any thing, he would not have escaped the sportsman.

On a person indebted for safety to his insignificance or trifling character. In the Egyptian dialect الشي الفلانة فاتني "such a thing has escaped me;" "I have not been able to lay hold of it."

582.*

لعن الله الحمام الذي ابصرتني است من لا اشتهي انظر وجهه

Cursed be the bath that has shown to me the hinder part of him whose face (even) I should not like to see.

Accident has thrown us into the society of one whose very aspect is disagreeable to us.

583.

لحمها و لحمه ما ينضاجوا في قدر

Her meat and his meat cannot be cooked together in the (same) pot.

Said of a husband and wife ill-suited to each other. ينضج "the preparing of victuals." In this sense also يستوي is used by the Egyptians.

584.

لو كانت تمطر كانت غيمت

If it were to rain, clouds would have appeared.

585.*

للسبع ما حازت يده

To the lion belongs whatever his hand has seized.

586.*

لو لا الدموع احترقت الضلوع

Were it not for the tears the ribs would have been burnt.

Tears soothe the pangs of distress.

587.*

ليس الفرس بجله و برقعه

The mare is not (to be valued) according to its housings and its ornaments in front.

جل the housings of a horse. The word برقع is used to denote the ornaments of a horse's head and foreparts.

588.

ليس في سقر حيث لا ما و لا شجار

(*He is*) *not in hell where neither water nor trees* (*can be found*).

A reply to those who bewail without reason the situation of another person. سقر is one of the upper regions in the Mohammedan hell.

589.

لو وقعت من السما صفعة ما سقطت الّا علي قفاه .

If a blow were to fall from heaven it would not ·light upon anything but his neck.

Said of the unfortunate. (Respecting a blow on the neck among the Egyptians and Arabs, see No. 2.)

590.

لو اتجرت في الاكفان لما مات احد

If I were to trade in winding-sheets, no one would die.

On a person unfortunate in commercial speculations.

591.*

ليس كل مَن سوّد وجهه قال انا حدّاد

Not every one whose face has been blackened can say "I am a blacksmith."

592.

لسان التجربة اصدق

The tongue of experience has most truth.

593.*

لو بلغ الرزق فاه لولّاه قفاه

*If the gain were to approach his mouth, he would
turn his back to it.*

Said of the negligent and indolent. قفا signifies
not only the hinder part of the neck, but also the
back.

594.

لا تمدنّ للمعالي يدا قصرت عن المعروف

*A hand that has been short in rendering services to
others, do not stretch it out in quest of high
places.*

The selfish person is unworthy of a high station.
لا تمدن the final ن strengthens the imperative, and
is called by the Arabs نون التاكيد By المعروف is
expressed " the rendering of kind services to
others;" such good offices as every one feels it his
duty to perform towards his fellow creatures. The
term in this sense is very commonly used; thus
تعمل معي معروف " will you be kind enough," whenever the services of a superior or inferior in rank are
solicited.

595.*

لا يقرا الّا اية العذاب و كتاب الصواعق

*He reads nothing but the sentences of torments and
the book of thunderbolts.*

Said of a person who always frightens others
with disastrous or portentous news. اية العذاب are
those passages of the Koran which threaten the
wicked with hell-torments. كتاب الصواعق alludes to
a work written by Ibn Hadjar (بن حجر) which has
for its title "The burning Thunderbolts" الصواعق
المحرقة—Ibn Hadjar is an author much esteemed
among the Olemas of Cairo ; several of his works on
the Hadyth or Tradition (especially his Annotations
to Kastellany's Commentary on the Hadyth,) serve
as guides in the lectures delivered at the Mosque el
Azhar.

596.

لا يسقط من كفّه الخردلة

*Not a single grain of mustard seed falls from his
hands.*

Said of the care with which a miller watches his
property. Mustard seed is extremely small.

597.

لا توخّر عمل اليوم لغد

Do not put off the work of this day till to-morrow.

يوخّر "to defer," "put back," &c.

598.*

لا تامن الامير اذا غشّك الوزير

Do not trust the emir if his vizir cheat thee.

599.

لا تلد الحية الّا حويّة

The serpent brings forth nothing but a little serpent.

600.

لا يشكر الله مَن لا يشكر الناس

Who gives not thanks to men, gives not thanks to God.

601.*

لا تسخر بكوسج ما لم يلتحي

Do not ridicule the short and thin-bearded, as long
as thou thyself art without a beard.

For كوسج the Egyptians more frequently say
كوسة   In ما لم the *ma* stands for ما زمان or ما طول

602.*

لا يفزع البازي من صياح الكركي

The hawk is not frightened by the cries of the crane.

It is not size that imparts courage or strength.
البازي is a species of buzzard common in Egypt and
Syria.   الكركي see No. 3.

603.

لا يجد في السما مصعدا و لا في الارض مقعدا

He finds no ascent to heaven and no seat on earth.

Said of one so perplexed and embarrassed that he knows not where to turn.

حرف الميم

604.

مَن دق الباب سمع الجواب

Who knocks at the door will hear the answer.

605.

ما كل ما يَعلم يُقال

All that is known is not told.

606.

مصايب قوم عند قوم فوايد

The misfortunes of some people are advantages to others.

607.*

ما الحزينة الثكلي كَالنايحة بكراها

*The afflicted mother who has lost her children is not
like the woman who weeps for hire.*

For نايحة the Egyptians now use the word ندّابة
to express those hired "pleureuses," or mourners.

608.

ما يعرف في السماء الا سهيل

*He does not know in the heavens any thing but
Sirius.*

He knows only the most conspicuous part of
heaven. A saying applied to persons little versed
in the details of business.

609.

ماجنون و عطي دستور

A fool—and free license was allowed.

The word دستور in Arabic has two significations.
It means, as here, the liberty granted to a person
who is high in favour to do whatever he pleases, a
circumstance usually the case with Turkish governors' favourites. It is also used as an exclamation
on entering the houses of strangers, and passing by
the places occupied by women, that they may be
warned to retire; it then is equivalent to "with
your leave," or "take care;" and in this sense it is
frequently employed.

610.*

ما كل وجه يقال له مرحبا

Not to every face is said " Welcome."

In Egypt مرحبا implies "welcome." In the
Hedjáz it means "you are welcome to it," or "I
am ready for it," and is the usual reply given by
servants when commanded to do any thing by their
masters. In Egypt the servant says on that occasion حاضر "I am ready."

611.

ما للجنازة حامية قال كل انسان ييكي علي حاله

" Why is the funeral so hot ? " *One answered,*
" Every person weeps for his own (unhappy)
state."

ما للجنازة is here used in the same manner as
ما لك (see No. 520,) and signifies "what is the
matter with the funeral," &c. A burial or funeral
is said to be حامية hot, or warm, when crowds of
mourners attend it, crying loudly. The women on
those occasions wave their handkerchiefs with both
hands over their heads, and following the bier, sing
the praises of the deceased, whom, whether male or
female, they celebrate chiefly for beauty or finery :—
" What a beautiful turban he had!" " What a
lovely person she was !" "What a fine veil she
wore !"

612.

ما يعرف حَرَّ الحَمَّام اَلَّا مَن دخلها

He alone knows the heat of the bath who has entered it.

613.

ما يضيع حق و خلفه مطالب

No right is lost which is followed up by demands.

614.

ما يبقي علي المداود اَلَّا شر البقر

The bad cows only remain at the mangers.

Said of those who continue as burthens on their families or friends. The good cows are either sold or employed in the field. مداود is the plural of مدود "a manger."

615.

ما كل مَن نفخت طبخت

It is not every woman who blows (the fire) that cooks also.

It may likewise mean "not every woman who puffs herself up or assumes airs;" for the word ينفخ may be used figuratively in Arabic as in English.

616.

ما كل معوَّج الرقبة جمل

Every thing crooked-necked is not a camel.

617.

ما كل جنّي يدخل القنينة

It is not every spirit that enters the glass bottle.

We cannot persuade or compel every person to
serve our purposes. Sorcerers who pretend to con-
fine hostile or familiar spirits in a glass bottle (قنينة)
are as well known in the East as in Europe.

618.

ما تمّ فولة مسوّسة الّا لها كيال اعور

*No worm-eaten bean remains without finding a
half-blind measurer.*

Every bad thing finds something equally bad to
match it. The word تمّ is frequently used in the
sense here expressed, as تمّ قاعد "he remained sitting;" تمّ يشتم حتّي "he continued railing or abusing
until—"

619.

من حسن لفظها بعتوها تخطب

*On account of her fine talking they sent her to woo
(for a friend).*

Said ironically of a woman who spoke in a mean
or vulgar manner. بعت according to the Egyptian
dialect for بعث

620.

من استحي من بنت عمه ما خاب منها غلام

He who is bashful with his cousin, gets no boy by her.

This saying is often addressed to a friend whon

we entreat to render us some service, or to pay a
debt. If we are ashamed, or act bashfully with him,
we obtain nothing from him. It is a general custom
in the Levant to marry the first cousin, and here
this name stands for " wife." Cousins thus married
continue to call each other " cousins," even after the
marriage, and not " husband and wife ; " because the
tie of first-cousinship is universally regarded as more
sacred than that of matrimony, which may be, and
is frequently, dissolved at the momentary caprice of
either party. Thus the man calls his wife in the
house يا بنت عمي " O daughter of my uncle ; " and
the wife says to her husband يا ابن عمي " O son of
my uncle."

621.

شبه ديوك العرب ياكل خرا و يدّن لله

*He is like the cocks of the Bedouins, eating dung and
calling to prayers gratis.*

Said of one who is left, notwithstanding all his
services, to live in poverty and contempt. The cock
is likened to the *muezzin*, because he crows at the
time of morning prayers when the muezzin calls the
people to their devotions. يدّن is the Egyptian
pronunciation of يوذّن The phrase " for God's sake,"
or " gratis," is expressed by لله The Bedouins (here
designated by the word *Arab*,) have no criers or
muezzins but their cocks.

622.

ما صاحت البقرة الّا للقاضي

None got the cow but the kádhy.

The arbitrator himself seized upon the object of dispute. صمّ لك is an expression frequently used, meaning "thou hast luckily gotten it," "it was exactly what thou shouldest have had," "it fell appropriately to thy lot." صمّ لك (from the verb يصمّ) originally signifies "it is perfect for thee."

623.

مَن يكون امه الحمّي و ابوه الباردة من اين تجيه العافية

To him whose mother is the hot fever, and whose father is the cold fever, from whence can health come?

Children suffer from the discordant tempers of their parents. تجيه in the Egyptian dialect for تجي له

624.

ما يخرج الزيت الّا المعصار

No one extracts the oil but the oil-presser.

To every sort of labour its own particular workman. المعصار is the person who works at the معصرة or oil-mill.

625.

مَن خَلَّف ما مات

He who leaves (the fame of good or great works) after him, does not die.

626.

مكبّة و جارية علي بجديد بسارية

*A covered dish and a handmaid for a farthing's
worth of sprats.*

The construction is مكبّة و جارية علي بسارية بجديد
the inversion is for the sake of the rhyme at the end.
مكبّة is the copper cover placed over the most choice
dishes in setting them before the guests. The
female slave is here supposed to bring one of those
dishes into the room, a great honour conferred upon
the company and upon the dish she carries, because
female slaves attend only on extraordinary occasions.
The small fishes called بسارية very much resemble
sprats of from two to four inches long; they are
found in the tanks and ponds of Egypt after the
inundation subsides. In these ponds the fish of the
Nile deposit their spawn; and when the river sinks,
the fishermen stop up the communication between it
and the ponds until the water becomes so shallow
that they can take the young fry in immense quan-
tities, by means of wicker baskets dragged along the
bottom. In order to feed the young fish, or *bisarye*,
they throw oil-cakes called *bokma* (بقمة) (made of
the dregs of hemp oil,) into the ponds, and this
fattens them in a short time. At present the
government has declared the whole fishery a public
concern, and lets it out to several companies. In
November and December the *bisarye* form one of
the principal dishes of the middling classes at Cairo,
and one pennyworth of them is sufficient to satisfy

a person. The original name of the *bisarye*, as I
have heard, is رضاضي Of the جديد (an ancient
copper coin of Egypt) few now remain, they being
no longer current; ten of them were equal to one
para. The preposition علي is put here for لاجل and
in this sense is often used; thus in the common
question "for what?" or "what for?" علي اي
stands for لاي سبب or لاي اجل

627.

ما بقي يعوز من النّقل آلا الزعرور

He wants of dried fruits only the zaroor.

Said of unreasonable demands. The بقي is here
a superfluous particle, as already noticed. (See
No. 263.) النقل are "dried fruits" (and النقلي "the
seller of dried fruits"). *Zarour* is a small fruit
resembling a cherry in size, and an apple in taste
and colour. It grows upon a low thorny shrub in
different parts of Syria, where I have seen it, especially in the Valley of the Jordan. I believe that it
is not a native of Egypt, and it is rarely to be found
in the shops of those Damascus people who sell dried
fruits at Cairo.

628.

ما قدر علي حماته قام لامراته

*He was not a match for his mother-in-law—he then
rose against his wife.*

Finding the actual enemy too powerful, he

attacks the weak and innocent. In the Egyptian dialect انا اقدر عليه signifies "I am quite a match (or an overmatch) for him." ما اقدر عليه "I am not a match for him." Instead of علي امراته we find لامراته—according to the practice before mentioned of putting the ل for علي—and vice versa.

629.

ما كفي الميّت موتته حتي عصره القبر

Death was not sufficient for the dead, the grave moreover must press upon him.

It is believed by Mohammedans that the tomb presses upon the body therein deposited either lightly or heavily according to the sins or merits of the deceased. This saying therefore means "not only was he punished for his sins by death, but the very tomb pressed upon him." Here حتي means "moreover," or "even,"—زيادة علي ذلك—having no reference to time. Thus it is said شتمه حتي ضربه "he abused him and even (or moreover) struck him."

630.

ما تتمّ الحيلة الّا علي الشطّار

The fraud is not complete unless it be practised upon clever and cunning persons.

It requires no ability to cheat the stupid. شطّار is the plural of شاطر "able," "active," and also "knowing and expert in business."

631.

ما يدخل الدرهم الزغل الا علي الصيرفي الزكي

False coin is passed upon none but the shrewd banker.

The over-shrewd are most easily cheated. يدخل عليه "it enters upon him;" that is, "it is passed upon him." The money-changers (صَيرِفِي) in Egypt are mostly Jews. In Syria, especially at Aleppo, these seyrafs, or bankers, are depositories of the cash of all the wealthy merchants. Each has in his shop a kind of Giro-bank, where sums of money are paid and received by his transferring them from one account book to another. This system much facilitates payments, and is conducted with sufficient security.

632.

مثل العتّال الميشوم ما يذكر الله الا تحت الحمل

(He is) like the perverse porter who calls upon God only when he is under the load.

He never thinks of God but when he is suffering from misfortune. The porters are accustomed to exclaim at every step while they carry heavy burthens, "O God! O God!" يا الله يا الله A porter or the carrier of a load is called in Egypt عتّال also شيَال or حَمال

633.

مَن تحبّه مِن اولادك قال مَن يدي علي كس اُمّه

"Which dost thou most love of thy children?" "That one," he replied, "whose mother's conduct I most strictly watch."

The father loves most that child of whose mother's fidelity he does not entertain a doubt. It must be recollected that in consequence of a plurality of wives the children of different beds are often found in one man's house. The Arabic scholar will easily perceive that the latter part of this proverb would not decently bear a literal translation.

634.

ما زرتني و انت جاري تجي من مصر علي حماري

Thou didst not visit me, and thou art my neighbour, (and) comest from Cairo upon my jackass.

Said of a person deficient in polite attentions towards those who had a right to expect them from him.

635.

موت المراة تجديد العرس

The death of the wife is the renewal of the wedding.

Here is an allusion to the custom of taking a new wife immediately on the death of a former. So universally is this practised, that no blame whatever is attached to a man or woman who remarry—

the former in the next fortnight, the latter after the
stipulated term of forty days, from the death of their
partners.

636.

مَن صَيَّر نفسه نُخالة اكلته البقر

Him who makes chaff of himself, the cows will eat.

He who does not support his own dignity will
be slighted and ill-treated. No Levantine will read
this sentence without exclaiming " *El hamdoo l'
illahy!* " "Thanks be to God! that is not my
foible!"

637.

مَن غاب غاب نصيبه

*He who absents himself loses his share (or his share
absents itself).*

That thou mayst prosper, attend to thy task.
نصيب " the lot bestowed by fate," also " a share or
portion."

638.

مزَين فتح باقرع استفتح

*A barber opened (his shop)—the first person whom he
shaved was scald-headed.*

Said of business commenced inauspiciously. مزَين
" a barber," the same as حلاق —after فتح is understood
دكانه " he opened his shop." In the Egyptian dialect
استفتَح is for افتتَح " to begin with ; " and the word is
generally used by shopkeepers to express the first

sale they make in the morning. Thus they say, " I
sold it cheap to you, that I might begin (this day's
sale) with a goodly work."

انا بعته لكم رخيص حتي استفتح بخير

639.

مفلس و مرابي ما اختلفوا

A bankrupt and an usurer do not disagree.
They easily conclude a bargain.

640.*

من طبخ شي ردي ياكل منه

He who cooks a bad thing, eats of it.

The promoter or contriver of a bad affair suffers
from it.

641.*

من هي عويشة في سوق الغزل

Who is Oweyshe in the market of the cotton-yarn?

A person great or famous in his own immediate
neighbourhood, is lost when he enters the crowd
upon the stage of this world. عويشة is a diminutive
of عيشة a woman's name. The diminutive is often
applied to the names of children who are favourites
with their parents or acquaintances. Every morning,
just after sunrise, the women of the lower classes at
Cairo take the cotton-yarn, which they have spun
at home, for sale to certain bázárs (سوق الغزل), where

of course there are great crowds of women, and
where Oweyshe, however eminent in her own quarter, is not distinguished from the others. The sale
of this yarn is one of the few means by which
females can earn an honest livelihood at Cairo, and
an industrious woman may support herself by
spinning.

642.

مَن رادكَ زيده و مَن طلب بعدكَ زيده

*Who likes thee, like him; and who wishes thee at a
distance, wish him at a still greater distance.*

زيده literally "give him more." Here is to be
understood زيده في طلب البعد Of a similar meaning
is the following proverbial saying :

مَن فاتكَ فوته و لا لكَ بهلقاه حاجة و مَن باعكَ بدينار
بيعه ببيضة دجاجة

*Who abandons thee, abandon him, for surely thou
hast no occasion to meet him; and who sold thee
for a dínár, sell him for a hen's egg.*

The Egyptians say راد and يريد in the same
sense as يحب—thus, فلان يريدني "such a one likes
me," or "is fond of me."

643.

مَن لا يستحي يعمل ما يشتهي

He who is not ashamed does whatever he likes.

644.*

مَن عاشر قوم اربعون صباح صار منهم

*He who intimately frequents people for forty days,
has become one of their number.*

صباح is often used instead of يوم

645.

ما يصعب الحق اآ علي الاحمق

Truth becomes disagreeable to the fool only.

646.

مَن اكل وحده غَص وحده

He who eats alone, coughs alone.

The egotist or selfish miser is abandoned in his
misfortunes. غَص to cough with the throat crammed,
or when one has been almost suffocated by something sticking in the windpipe. It is reckoned a
shame in the East to eat alone, and those who do so
are despised as misers.

647.

ما هذا بيت الفرس

This is not the bishop's square.

This is not the proper place for a person. A
saying derived from the chess-board, where the
square is called بيت or "house."

648.

ماشطة و تمشط بنتها

*A hair dresser, and she combs (or dresses the hair
of) her daughter.*

This is said of good work, such as is executed by
skilful artists when they work " con amore." ماشطة
among the peasants signifies " a woman who earns
her livelihood by combing and cleaning the long
thick hair of the female villagers, which she afterwards plaits," an operation to which all the respectable Turkish women submit at least once in every
week. This business is performed in towns at the
baths by professional women called بلانة

649.

ما اكثر خطّابي و ما اقل فراشي

*How very great is the number of my wooers; but
how small the quantity of my furniture.*

A pretty girl, but too poor to obtain a husband.
الفراش comprises the whole furniture—beds, sofas,
kitchen utensils, china-ware, &c. which a wife brings
to her husband, amounting often to a greater value
than the price paid for the girl to her father. She
retains, however, the property of this furniture,
unless she demands a divorce, when the husband
may claim it on her leaving his house.

650

ما حد يَحقَر روحه

Nobody considers himself as contemptible.

In the Egyptian dialect حد is used for أحد—
and روحه commonly for نفسه

651.

من تكلّم في ما لا يعنيه سمع ما لا يرضيه

He who talks about that which does not concern him,
will hear something not pleasing to him.

652.*

ما علي القلوب دروب

How many are the roads that lead not to the heart!

ما is here to be understood as يا ما

653.

ما في الفاخورة مثله

Among the pottery there is none like him.

He is distinguished only among his low companions.

654.

مَن لا يصل للعنقود يقول عليه حامض

He who cannot reach to the bunch of grapes, says
of it, "It is sour."

655.

مَن تصدق بالنخال كتب له علي الصراط الصراط

He who distributes bran in alms, for him it is written in the Book of Destiny that he is to receive a puff of wind upon the serât.

The serât is that narrow bridge by which the Moslims pass over the precipice of Hell towards the avenues of Paradise.

656.

مَن تزوّج في سوق الطير كان طلاقه تمسوا بالخير

Of him who marries in the bird-market, the divorce will be (as quick as one can say) "good night."

Women of the lower class and of unchaste character sell pigeons and other birds in the different bázárs of Cairo. Here is to be understood كان طلاقه كقول تمسوا بالخير That a person went off in haste, is expressed thus, قال تمسوا بالخير و راح "he said 'good evening,' and went away." In the East on quitting a company it is not usual to make long adieus; a man says merely "good night," or "good morning," and immediately withdraws. The proverb may perhaps also mean, that if the person marries in the morning at the bird-market he will be divorced on the evening of the same day.

657.

مِن اوّل الخلّ دَردِي

From the beginning of the vinegar dregs were in it.

The affair was badly concerted from the first. دَردِي in the Egyptian dialect signifies "dregs or lees," the same as عكر

658.

مثل الدنيا ما فيه اعتقاد

(He is) like the world; no confidence is to be placed in him.

659.

مثل ما تعمل الشاة في القَرَض يعمل القرض في جلدها

As the sheep does with the acacia-pulse, the acacia-pulse does with the sheep's skin.

قرض is the fruit of the mimosa called سَنط or صَنط consisting of a small pulse or pod resembling that of carobs. It contains several beans, and when fresh is excellent food for cattle; when dried it is used by the tanners in Upper Egypt and all the Bedouins of Arabia to tan sheep's skins.

660.

مكتوب علي ورق الخيار مَن سهر الليل نام النهار

It is written upon the cucumber leaf, "He who watches during the night sleeps during the day."

He who passes the night in revelry is unfit for

business during the day. *"It is written upon the cucumber leaf,"* signifies that it is written where even the meanest people may read it, as cucumbers are very cheap and common in Egypt. الليل and النهار are here put for باللتل and بالنهار or في الليل In this manner the Egyptians frequently dispense with the prepositions بي and في

661.

ما في جهنم مراوح

There are no fans in hell.

مراوح the plural of مروحة "a fan made of the chips of date-leaves."

662.

مَن فاته اللحم فلياكل من المرق

He who loses an opportunity of (eating) the meat, let him feed on the broth.

An Arabian story relates that the bird *kombar* (قنبر of the lark species,) once invited King Solomon to dine, and requested that all his courtiers might accompany him. The king inquired whether there was a sufficient supply of food for so large a company; and received in answer, that everything necessary had been provided. The guests arrived and seated themselves near the banks of a river; when dinner time approached the kombar came flying with a locust in his bill. Having eaten some

of it himself, he threw the rest into the water, and
addressed this proverb to his royal guest, advising
him to satiate himself with the locust-broth. The
wise monarch smiled, he and his attendants drank
some of the water, thanked their host, and departed.

663.

مَن كلّم الزُّطِّي عليْ نفسه يِخْطِي

He who talks with the Zotty commits a sin against
himself.

Avoid the conversation of unmannerly persons.
زُطِّي an Arabian tribe noted for the coarseness of
their manners. I have heard at Cairo, (but cannot
affirm as fact,) that a small tribe of Zotty is still
established in some villages of Palestine.

664.*

ما بقي بعد عَبَّادان قريةٌ

After Abbádán no village remains (or exists).

This is said in derision of the praises which
people so lavishly bestow upon their native places,
even the most miserable hamlets. *Abbádán* (عَبَّادان)
was a place on the eastern bank of the Tigris,
belonging to the district of *Sowád*. I am ignorant
whether *Abbádán* exists at present or not; nor can
I imagine why the Egyptians should have introduced it into one of their proverbial sayings. قرية
signifies a village in the modern dialect of Egypt.

665.

ما في المعدية واحد لله

*There is not in the ferry boat any (gratis or) for
God's sake.*

There every person must pay his fare. لله is used
in the same manner as the expression "for God's
sake," i.e. *gratis.*

666.

ما يملا عين ادم الَا التراب

The dust alone can fill the eye of man.

Man continues to be ambitious or covetous until
he is deposited in the dust. Common expressions
are عينه مليان (for عينه ملان) "his eye is full," or
"he possesses every object of his desire, he is
satiated;" دا ما يملا عينه "this does not fill his eye,"
or content him. This figurative sense is restored in
the proverb to the real meaning of "to fill the eye."
تراب here signifies تراب القبر the "dust of the
grave." A saying of Mohammed resembling this
proverb in sense is recorded as follows:—

لا يملا جوف بن ادم الَا التراب

667.*

من له راس عند الرواس ما ينام الليل

*He who has a head at the sellers of sheep's heads,
does not sleep at night.*

The person whose fortune is intrusted to the

hands of strangers, cannot enjoy repose. The poor
at Cairo buy sheep's heads and for a trifle have
them boiled in the bázár by persons who are not
only cooks, but sellers of sheep's heads, and therefore called رُاس, or in the Egyptian dialect رَوّاس

668.

مَن لا تاكل في فرحه كله في عزاه

*Of that person at whose wedding thou dost not eat,
eat at the funeral.*

Lose no opportunity of gaining from a stingy
person. The more natural construction of this proverb would be

الذي لا تاكله الكل في فرحه كله في عزاه

The word عزا means the first days of mourning
after a person's death, generally spent by his relations in loud expressions of grief; sumptuous entertainments being given to the mourners. Instead of
عزا the Egyptians say also مينم which is a corruption
of ماتم

669.

من تعب استراح

He who is fatigued shall repose (afterwards).

استريح is the expression used in inviting a person
to sit down when he enters a room, as the Arabs say
اجلس

670.

ما لي بقر و لا قوم ساحر

I have no cows, nor do I set myself up as a sorcerer.

I have no money left to assist thee (or to supply the want of thy lost cow). اقوم "I rise" (to do or to be), "I suddenly begin to be."

671.

من لا يرضي بحكم موسي رضي بحكم فرعون

He who is not satisfied with the government of Moses, will be satisfied with the government of Pharaoh.

This saying has latterly been often quoted to express that those who did not like the Mamelouks, must now submit to the still more tyrannical government of Mohammed Aly. The construction is according to the vulgar dialect of Cairo, it should have been (more correctly)

من لم رضي بحكم موسي يرضي بحكم فرعون

672.

ما هو الّا نار المجوس

It is nothing but the fire of the Magians.

Said to a person who highly values that which finally must hurt him. The Madjous, or Idolaters, adore the same element which burns them.

673.*

مَن لا يذق اللحم اعجبته الرِّية

*He who does not taste the (best part of the) meat
likes the lungs.*

The poor must be content with that which the
rich disdains. The lungs are eaten only by the
poor. Instead of رية the Egyptians more commonly
use the term فِشّة in speaking of lungs.

674.

مَن كان طبّاخه ابو جعران ما عسي تكون الالوان

*Of him whose cook is a beetle, what may not be
the dishes?*

What can the work be if slovenly fools are
employed to execute it? ابو جعران is the largest
species of خنفسة or scarabæus, and cited, like the
latter, as an emblem of ugliness and filth. It is the
same animal which the learned Arabians sometimes
call جُعَل

675.

من اكل للسلطان فرخة ردّها له بقرة

*He who eats a hen of the sultan will return her
to him a cow.*

On the heavy fines imposed on those who em-
bezzle the public money. اكل is constantly used to
imply "the taking of illegal gain." Thus اكل مني
"he has cheated me;" اكل من الفلوس "he has eaten
(embezzled) some of the money." But it always
supposes that the eater has betrayed at the same

time the trust or confidence placed in him. Therefore it is not said of a shopkeeper who cheats his
customer by overcharges منه اكل—but غشّه " he
cheated him ;" but if my servant overcharges me in
an account of my expenses, I say اكل مني " he has
cheated me."

676.*

من لا يصلاحه التخير لا يصلاحه الشر

*Him whom goodness cannot mend, evil will not
mend.*

On such incorrigible persons as cannot be
softened by kindness nor corrected by punishment.
On this subject the following verse is cited :—

اذا كان الطباع طباع سوٍ

فلا ادبٌ يعيد و لا اديب

677.

من احب شي اكثر من ذكرة

He who loves a thing often talks of it.

Literally "abounds in the mentioning of it."

678.

مَن يقدر علي ردّ امس و تطيين عين الشمس

*Who is able to restore (what was) yesterday, or
to plaster over the rays of the sun?*

One is as impossible as the other. This is
generally said of any undertaking quite beyond the

reach of human power. تطيين (from طين) to cover a wall or anything with mud, plaster, &c.

679.

مِن العجايب اعمش كتحال

Among wonderful things is a sore-eyed person who is an oculist.

A man should first attend to his own defects. In Egypt those quacks are styled كتحال who pretend to cure the eyes, for which purpose they usually employ a mixture of mineral or metallic substances, especially antimony, and from this they derive their name.

680.

ما المرو الّا بدرهميه

Man is only man by his money.

This vile saying is in opposition to the celebrated answer given to the great Arab chief, or King of Hyra, Noman Ibn Monzer, by his enemy and rival Dhamra Ibn Dhamra, whom Noman when he came into his presence reproached for the meanness of his look and the smallness of his person. The noble Bedouin replied, "Surely the worth of a man lies in two of his smallest parts—his heart and his tongue!"

انما المرو باصغريه قلبه و لسانه

Others affirm that this answer was given by the Arab Mady Kerb to the King of Persia.

681.

مني اتفرزنت يا بيدق

When wert thou changed into a queen, O pawn?

Said of low people suddenly elevated. This is taken from the chess board, when a pawn passes to queen (فرز). The ١ of اتفرزنت is superfluous, and must be ascribed merely to the vulgar pronunciation. The ancient poet Abou Tamam has a similar expression :

فرزنتم سرعة ما اري يا بيدق

682.*

من اكل مرقة السلطان احترقت شفتاه و لو بعد حين

Of him who eats the sultán's broth, the lips will be scalded, should it be even at a very distant time.

On the dangers attending those who accept lucrative situations under Eastern rulers. The اكل is here in its true sense and implies "illegal eating," or "gain." من مرقة السلطان stands for مرقة Thus it is said انا ياكل عيشه "I ate *of* his bread," as if من preceded عيشه or as a host says to his guest, كل اللحم "eat *of* the meat," for كل من اللحم

حرف النون

683.

نواية تسند الحجرة

A small date-stone props up the water-jar.

Great princes often owe their security to the meanest of their subjects; or, great concerns are supported by the most trifling circumstances. نواية is the diminutive of نوي That the large water-jars, which are of this form—

may be kept in an upright position and well balanced, some small stones are often put under them.

684.

ناصح الاحمق عدوه

The adviser of the fool is (or becomes) his enemy.

The word احمق is applied in Egypt not only to a fool, but also to an obstinate headstrong person.

685.

ناكوها سكتت عاتبوها تغنّجت

*They embraced her, she remained silent; they re-
proached her, then she assumed airs.*

She dreads the reproach, but is not ashamed of
the deed. ينيک "to enjoy female society." تغنّجت
from غنج which signifies "the twisting of the body
and coy motions of a woman impatient of reproach."
The same word is often used to express similar
motions produced by coquetry or voluptuousness,
and the women of Cairo flatter themselves that their
غنج is superior to that of all other females in the
Levant.

686.

نفّاخة الاسطبل

The blowing of the stable.

This is said on two occasions; first, when a
person resembles a horse that issues from his stable
in full vigour, snorts and breathes high, blows out
at the nostrils, and strikes the ground with his
hoofs, but soon after is found to be tired; secondly,
it is applied to a person resembling the grooms of
the stable, who puff themselves up and give themselves great airs, fellows noted in Egypt for their
insolence.

687.

نار الحلفا سريعة الانطفا

The fire of reeds is of rapid extinction.

The passions of those who have no energy of character are easily subdued.

688.*

نشا مع نوح في السفينة

He was born with Noah in the ark.

Of ancient origin, of long standing.

689.*

الانسان عبد الاحسان

Man is the slave of beneficence.

Beneficent actions and kindnesses enslave a man to the generous.

690.

نزلتّ منه بوادي غير ذي زرع

I alighted (at his house) in a barren valley.

Said of an inhospitable mansion, in allusion to a passage of the Koran (Chapter xiv), wherein it is said

ربنا اني اسكنت من ذرّيتي بوادٍ غير ذي زرع

by which valley is understood the valley of Mekka. منه stands here for عنده or فيه—these prepositions being in common conversation frequently misused one for the other.

691.

النصح بين الملا تقريع

Advice given in the midst of a crowd is loathsome.

الملا the (place) filled (with people). تقريع in the
Egyptian dialect "loathsomeness," "disgust," &c.
This meaning is well expressed by an ancient poet,
as follows :

و اذا وجدتّ علي الصديق شكوته سرًّا و في المحافل اشكرّ

If I should find my friend in the wrong, I reproach
him secretly; but in presence of company, I
praise him.

692.

لناس بزمانهم اشبه منه باباييهم

People resemble still more the time in which they
live, than they resemble their fathers. (Verbatim
—Men, with their time, are more similar to it,
than to their fathers.)

This proverb means, that the general state of
society, its notions and manners, have more influence
upon man than education or the example set by his
parents. A maxim equally just as sagacious. It
might have been expressed more precisely in Arabic
thus—

شبه الناس بزمانهم اكثر من مشابهتهم لاباييهم

693.

النَّاي في كُمّي و الريح في فَمّي

The clarionet is in my sleeve and the breath in my mouth (ready for playing).

Used to express " I am completely ready for business." نَاي is a sort of clarionet very common in the Levant.

694.

نظر الشحيح الي الغريم المفلس

(Like) the look of the miser at his bankrupt debtor.

حرف الهآ

695.

هدايا الاحباب علي ورق السداب

The presents of our friends are (as dear to us as if they were) upon the leaves of rue.

It is well known that presents are frequently interchanged between friends in the East. A thing is generally presented wrapped in a handkerchief, or placed on the leaves of some fragrant herbs or flowers. سداب is the plant *rue*, a favourite among

the Turks and Arabs, whose drawing-rooms often contain it in pots.   It is likewise called سنداب
Here we must understand كانها علي ورق

696.

هارب و يهلّل

He is running away, yet shouts loudly.

Instead of endeavouring to facilitate his escape by silence, he attracts notice by crying with a loud voice.   For يهلّل it is more usual to say يصرخ

697.

هات اليوم صوف و خذ غدا نعاج

Give me wool to-day, and take sheep to-morrow.

Applicable to those who give small presents hoping to receive some more valuable in return. This is almost universally the case where a Levantine makes a present to an European.

698.

هِته عاليه و بطنه خاليه

He is high-minded, but empty-bellied.

699.*

هو قدر الزر و يشغل السرّ

It is not larger than a button, yet it annoys us.

The merest trifles may cause vexation and pain.

زر is a silk button which fastens the gown about the neck. السر means here "the innermost, the secret, the mind, the secret intention." يشغل السر "it distresses and occupies our inmost thoughts, it vexes us;" so this expression is frequently used. Of the same sense is يتعب السر We hear also سره مشغول or سره تعبان "he is vexed." لا تتعب سري "do not vex me."

700.

هو طبل تحت كسا

Is this a drum hidden under the clothing?

The drum will be heard although it may be hidden. The question means, "Do you suppose that so awkward an attempt to conceal this mystery can hide it from the public?"

701.

هان المسك و انتثر حتي يستعملوه البقر

Musk became so common and was scattered about, so that even the cows used it.

Said of a precious thing used by mean people; or of a distinguished personage connected with those unworthy of his acquaintance.

702.

هو وجهك يا حزينة في الحلي و الزينة

It is thy face, O woman in grief, when ornamented and attired.

A reproof to an ugly woman angry at her face

and endeavouring to deck it with ornaments. This
saying is applied to all vain attempts at concealing
natural deformities or bad qualities.   حَلِي   means
"the jewels or gold and silver ornaments of the
the head or neck."   الزِينة   "whatever is used at a
woman's toilette for the purpose of personal decora-
tion;" such as the kohel for her eyes, the henna
for her fingers, the perfume for her hair, &c.

703.

هي صنعة بعقاقير

Is this an art of drugs?

Is it as difficult as the profession of a druggist?
This is said to imply that it is as a matter of which
the knowledge may be easily acquired.   عقاقير   in the
Egyptian dialect signifies all the different drugs,
spices, simples, &c., which are found in druggists'
shops, and which cannot well be distinguished one
from another without much skill and patience.

704.*

هو سم ساعة

It is an hour's poison.

It is of a very destructive quality, causing almost
immediate ruin.

705.

هي مَوْنة سنة

Is this provision for a year?

Said in advising a person not to squander away his little stock of provisions, and to regulate his expenses.

706.*

هذا الميّت لا يساوي البكا

This dead (person) is not worth the weeping.

707.

اهتك ستور الشك بالسوال

Tear off the curtain of doubt by questions.

Doubt is here personified as a veil or curtain with which virgin truth or knowledge is covered. In its original sense هتك signifies to remove the veil of a woman so that her face may be exposed. Hence are derived the other significations, disgracing and violating, certain consequences in the East attending the removal of a woman's veil by force.

708.*

وصل القطار للجميزه

The camels have reached the sycamore tree.

قطار is a line of camels walking one behind
another, each being fastened by its halter to the tail
of the one immediately before him. In the open
country of Egypt large sycamore trees are frequently
found by the side of public fountains (سبيل), under
the shade of which travellers and cattle often repose.

709.*

وصل السكين للعظم

The knife has reached the bone.

The wound is deep.

710.

وقف الباب علي عقبه

The door has rested upon its hinges.

Everything has been placed in its proper situation.

711.

وقع الفاس في الراس

The axe has fallen upon the head.

The blow was well directed.

712.

وريقة و انبلت

A small leaf, and it was wetted.

A poor little creature, and overwhelmed by misfortune.

713.

واحد حلق لحيته و الثاني ينتف شِعرته قالوا كل من هو

بشهوته

*One shaved his beard, a second plucked out his hairs;
every one, they said, according to his own liking.*

The abridged phrase كل مَن هو بشهوته is often
used in the same sense as "de gustibus non est
disputandum." هو stands for كان— to express it
clearly we should say, كل من كان فهو بشهوته Respecting the true meaning of شعرة see No. 202. Whenever the word *beard* is mentioned in the same
phrase with a term expressing some object dirty or
contemptible, it always implies disrespect or ridicule
towards the owner of the beard, this appendage so
venerated among the Arabs. Indeed they carry
their scruples respecting it to such a degree that
when a person relates a story or sings a song in
which occur the words dung, hogs, dogs, or other

terms denoting what they regard as filthy or impure,
he requests any of his auditors who may at that
moment be in the act of touching his beard or
moustaches, to remove his hand, which request
proves that no offensive allusion was meant between
the beard and the word which the speaker or singer
was going to pronounce.

714.

واحد ينيك امراته و جارته اتغنجت

*A person embraces his wife; a female neighbour
affects to look as if she herself were in the wife's
place.*

Said of a bystander who assumes the air of
enjoying that which he had merely happened to
witness. I have heard this proverb (which, as the
Arabic scholar will perceive, is not very literally
translated,) often quoted in respectable society.
And there are many others still more indelicate, not
inserted in this collection, although frequently used
by the best-bred people, even in the presence of
virtuous and most respectable women.

715.

وجه مليح و ياكل شيء قبيح

A fine face, but eats vile things.

Alluding to a person of good appearance who
commits base actions.

716.

وجوه كِشّة و قلوب غِشّة

Sour faces and deceitful hearts.

كِشّة in the Egyptian dialect, " a sour, morose,
ill-natured countenance," than which nothing is
more disliked in the East, where a man is forgiven
for being a scoundrel, but not if he seems to despise
or dislike scoundrels.

717.

وحش و يكشّ و يقعد في الوش

*Rude and morose, yet he sits in front (of the
company).*

He takes a place to which he is not entitled. I
have before remarked that the Orientals dislike
extremely a sour or morose countenance. وحش in
the dialect of Egypt is seldom used to express
savage or *wild*, but " rude in manners and appearance." يكش see No. 716. الوش so pronounced by
many persons for وج It is to be understood
في وش المجلس

718.

وجهه يقطع الرزق

His face cuts off all gain.

His face is so disagreeable that no one likes to
deal with him.

719.

وداه البحر و جابه ·عطشان

He led him to the river, yet brought him back thirsty.

ودي or يودي in the Egyptian dialect means "to carry, lead, transport, bring to." الي البحر for البحر or الي بحر النيل

720.*

وقعت منارة اسكندرية قال الله يسلّمنا من غبارها

The Pharos of Alexandria has fallen down. "God save us," said they, "even from the very dust of it."

The fall of a great man is to be dreaded, even in its remote consequences or effects.

721.

واحد قعد يتمنّي طلوع الصبح فلما طلع الصبح عمي

A person sat demanding as a favour from God the rise of morn—when morn arose, he became blind.

We have often to lament the accomplishment of our wishes; or when they are fulfilled we cannot enjoy them. This proverb is derived from the following verse—

فكان كالمتمنّي ان يري فلقًا
من الصباح فلما ان راه عمي

The verb قعد does not here exactly mean " he sat," but is employed as a kind of auxiliary, signifying nothing more than كان—thus, اقعد ساكت " be silent," or "sit silent," said to a person whether sitting or standing. قَعَد يَحدثني حتي "he did speak to me until"—or rather "he continued speaking to me until"—انا تعدت احبه زمان "I did love him for a long time," or "I continued loving him for a long time."

722.

اوهي من بيت العنكبوت

More easy to be broken than the house of the spider.

This is taken from the Koran, where we read,

و ان اوهن البيوت لبيت العنكبوت

723.

واحد علق ثور وقع قال رشوا عليه ماء قال حتي يطلع
شي نرشه عليه

A certain person tied an ox (to the water-wheel). The animal fell. "Sprinkle some water upon him," (said the man). "Let us first," replied one, "get some out of the well to sprinkle upon him."

Said in ridicule of foolish advisers. An ox is here supposed fastened to a wheel that draws up water from a well. علق is the technical term used by peasants to express "he tied the ox (to the wheel)." حتي يطلع شي to be understood as حتي يطلع شي ماء من البير

حرف اللام الف

724.

لا تزيد المبلّة طني

Do not add more mud to the Mobella.

Do not make an evil worse, nor add fuel to the fire. المبلّة is a tank sunk into the ground above four feet, and from forty to fifty feet square; it is walled up with stones and level with the surface of the ground : the floor is composed of unburnt mud bricks. In this tank the Egyptian peasants deposit their flax after it has been well dried in the sun. They then let in water and cover the wetted flax with heavy stones, leaving it in that condition until a sufficient state of maceration renders it fit for being worked. They find it necessary to keep this floor very clean, because the masses of clay would spoil the flax; hence arises the proverb. The *mo-bella* is also called معطنة—and to prepare the flax in this manner يعطن

725.*

لا تقطع في كيس غيرك

Do not cut out of the purse of another.

Do not seize upon that which does not belong to
thee. The people of Cairo say تطعتُ فولان—meaning
" I have unjustly or by force taken something away
from such a one." The word ضربة is used in the
same sense ; and they also say, لا تضرب في كيس غيرك

726.

لا عند ربّك و لا عند استاذك

It is neither (to be found) with thy God nor with
thy landholder.

It is in vain to ask for the thing, no one can
give it to thee. The Egyptian peasants call the land-
holders or proprietors of their fields by the name of
استان In towns those landlords are called ملتزم
But at present this class does not exist in Egypt,
as Mohammed Aly Pasha has sequestered all landed
property of individuals, and obliged them to take
from the fiscus what they formerly received as rents
from their farmers.

727.

لا ارافقك و لا اوافقك و لا افارقك

I will not be thy friend, nor will I suit thee, nor
will I leave thee.

This is said of a wearisome hanger-on, who
knows that he is disliked, yet perseveringly obtrudes

his presence upon his acquaintances. Persons of this description are numerous in the Levant. يرافق comes from رفيق a "companion," also a "friend." The proverb is derived from an old Arabian saying—

من البليّة صديقٌ يرافقك و لا يوافقك و لا يفارقك

728.

لا بعينك رايت و لا بقلبك حبيت

Neither with thine eye hast thou seen, nor with thy heart hast thou loved.

Applied to one who affects violent love for a person whom he has never seen unveiled.

729.

لا تعير الاحق شي يحسب انه له

Lend not to the fool anything, else he may fancy that it belongs to himself.

730.

لا ربح ثوابه و لا خلاه لاصحابه

He gained no merit (by spending it liberally) nor did he leave it to the right owners.

He unjustly took (the money) from another, without rendering it profitable to himself or any one else. لا ربح ثوابه here is to be understood لا ربح الثواب في التصدق "he gained not the merit of having expended it in alms."

731.

لا يغرّك رُخصه ترمي نُصّه

*Do not let its cheapness delude thee; thou wilt (if
thou purchase it) throw away half of it.*

According to the Egyptian pronunciation نصّ
is used for نصف although other words of the same
form are correctly pronounced, such as خصف—وصف
قصف—&c.

732.

لا تزال الحاجة الميشومة عند صاحبها حتي ياجي مَن يشتريها

*The bad stuff remains with its owner until
(some fool) comes to buy it.*

حاجة often means "a thing, some article of
merchandise, some stuff," &c.; it is frequently
synonymous with شي—thus, حط الحاجة في الصندوق
"put the thing into the chest." (See Nos. 34 and
378.)

733.*

لا صلح الّا بعد عداوة

There is no peace until after enmity.

734.

لا تعيّط في وجه الرزق يهرب

*Do not cry out in the face of gain else it flies
away.*

This is quoted as advice to dealers, that they

should behave civilly towards customers and not reject good offers harshly; otherwise the goods may remain upon their hands.

735.*

لا مليح و لا نفاق و لا طيب اخلاق

Neither handsome, nor liberal, nor good-natured.

Said of a repulsive character. نفاق one who expends money liberally.

736.*

لا تعامل بطّال و لا صاحب حمار

Have no dealings with the indolent, and none with the owner of the jackass.

The lazy will do nothing for thee; and the owner of the jackass will purchase food for his beast with the profits which he ought to divide with thee. معاملة signifies "trade," "commercial or pecuniary concerns." لا تعامله is equivalent to لا تجعل بينك و بينه معاملة

737.

لا تقدّم نحس تتعب في تاخيره

Do not push forward a worthless fellow, else thou wilt be tired in putting him back again.

738.

لا تضرب الديب و لا تجوع الغنم

*Do not beat the wolf, and do not cause hunger to
the sheep.*

Be kind and mild towards friends and enemies.
This is the only maxim recommending universal
charity that I have been able to discover among
those current at Cairo.

739.

لا علي في الكتاب و لا فاطمة في المعلمة

*(I have) neither an Aly in the reading school, nor a
Fatme in the working school.*

I am not encumbered with children and therefore ready for any vocation. The school كتّاب is
generally held in a mosque where little children
learn to read the Korán. After four or five years
they are sent to attend lectures in the mosque,
where the Korán is explained, and their language
and religion systematically taught, but little else.
معلمة is the school where women instruct young girls
in sewing and spinning. Among a thousand females
at Cairo scarcely one can be found who knows how
to read, and perhaps not more than twenty who
know how to pray or possess the least notion of
their religion. Even among the highest classes the
education of the mind is totally neglected.

740.

لا تعطي المنجّم في هذا فلوس

Do not give any money to the astrologer for this.

The expectations which the fortune-teller has excited in thy mind are ridiculous, and he is not entitled to any remuneration. منجّم an astrologer. Sheikhs and olemas are found in every town of Egypt, who deceive the credulous by their pretended skill in fortune-telling.

741.*

لا للسيف و لا للضيف

(A person good) neither for the sword nor for the guest.

Cowardly and stingy.

حرف اليآ

742.*

يَحتمل الدوا لمنفعته

We must bear the medicine on account of its usefulness.

743.

يركب بلاش و يغامز امراة الرّيس

*He gets his passage for nothing, and winks to the
wife of the captain (of the ship).*

He owes obligations to the captain, yet endeavours to seduce his wife. يركب here is to be
understood يركب المركب The word يغامز signifies
"to wink at," or "make mutual signals of intelli-
gence with another person." رِيّس in the Egyptian
dialect for رئيس

744.

يوجد في الاسقاطا ما لا يوجد في الاسفاطا

*Among things thrown away is found (perhaps) that
which is not found in the casket.*

سفط a box in which jewels and golden ornaments
are kept.

745.

يمرق من الزرد

He slips out through the coat of mail.

He is so full of wily tricks that he would con-
trive to slip away through the wire-work of a coat
of mail. The word يمرق is seldom used in Egypt,
but frequently in Syria, and in the Black country
on the Nile, and in Hedjáz, where to express "*be
gone,*" (or the vulgar English "*get out,*") امرق is
used; for which in Egypt the word اخرج is common.

746.

يعوم في شبر ماء

He swims in a span (depth) of water.

He is full of resources and knows how to avail
himself of the smallest means.

747.

يحتاج الذهب للنّخال

The gold wants bran.

The great want the assistance of the mean. Gold
is cleaned with bran.

748.

يا مطعمين اهل برّا و اهل جوا يشتهوه اتعدوا جنب
الطريق و كلوه

*O you who feed the people without while those within
are (left) longing for it, sit down out of the way
to eat it.*

This is said in advice to those who make an
ostentatious display of hospitality towards strangers,
but leave their own family to starve. جوا in the
Egyptian dialect "inside," "within." جنب الطريق
"by the side of the road where travellers pass," *viz.,*
out of their way. Eat with your own people.

It is very usual in the Levant to eat before the
gate of the house where travellers pass, and every
stranger of respectable appearance is invariably requested to sit down and partake of the repast.

Even the poorest man while he is eating invites any one passing by to share his humble meal. It must be acknowledged that with respect to food, the Egyptians, and in general the Orientals of every class, are generous towards strangers as well as towards the poor. I have reason to believe that very few at Cairo suffer from hunger, at least they may be certain of getting food in some part of the town before sunset; and those who feel for their fellow creatures must be gratified on reflecting when they retire to sleep, that in this great capital there are few, if any, individuals who pass the night without thanking God for an evening meal, although poor-houses, hospitals, parish-rates, and public charitable institutions, are here unknown. This consideration counterbalances a number of disadvantages, and tends to reconcile us with the character of the inhabitants and their political condition. Beggars can easily obtain work if they like to be employed, and they neither suffer from the inclemency of seasons nor from want of lodgings; all the lower classes being from their infancy accustomed to go half-naked and to sleep upon the bare ground under the canopy of heaven.

But on the other hand, this facility of procuring food is a main cause of inactivity and indolence among the Egyptians, which would be carried still farther did not the extortions of government oblige them to work, merely that they might pay the land taxes. It is not the southern sun, as Montesquieu imagines, but the luxuriance of southern soil, and the abundance of provisions, that relax the exertions of the inhabitants and cause apathy. Where a man is almost certain of finding sufficient food, however coarse or simple, he is easily tempted to indulge in laziness. By the fertility of Egypt, Mesopotamia, and India, which yield their produce almost spontaneously, the people are lulled into indolence; while in neighbouring countries, of a temperature equally warm, as among the mountains of Yemen and Syria, where hard labour is necessary to ensure a good harvest, we find a race as superior in industry to the former, as the inhabitants of Northern Europe are to those of Spain or Italy.

749.

يستقصي علي البشنين و من زرعه

He inquires about the Beshneen and the person who sowed it.

Everybody at Cairo knows the plant *beshneen*, and that it is not sown, but grows wild. يستقصي " to inquire," is a verb of very common use. The beshneen is undoubtedly the lotus of the ancient Egyptians; at least its flower resembles exactly the lotus as it is represented on the walls of the Egyptian temples. The flower consists of four green-coloured outer leaves, and four of a violet or rose colour placed in the interstices of the others; these inclose the inner part, which consists of a double set of smaller white leaves one behind another, in the midst of which stands the yellow seed-vessel, about one inch and a half high. The whole flower when half opened is one of the most beautiful plants in Egypt, which is probably the reason why the natives call these plants "the brides of the Nile" عرايس النيل It rests upon a stalk which is about three feet five inches long, covered externally with a green skin, under which lies a second skin of a fine violet colour, spotted with white. The children play with this stalk, the inside of which is fibrous, and use it as a pipe-tube by placing some lighted tobacco at the place where the seed-vessel stood, the smoke of this they draw through the stalk. In their hands it closely resembles the plant which is held by the Theban priests in the pictures that decorate their temples.

They likewise eat the yellow seed-vessel, of which the taste is not disagreeable, though rather insipid. The flower generally stands on the stalk from one foot to two feet above the surface of the water. When the flower opens completely the leaves form a horizontal disk, with the isolated seed-vessel in the midst, which bends down the stalk by its weight and swims upon the surface of the water for several days, until it is ingulphed. This plant grows at Cairo in the tank called *Birket el Rotoli*, near one of the northern suburbs, where I happened to reside. It is not found in Upper Egypt, I believe, but abounds in the Delta, and attains maturity at the time when the Nile reaches its full height. I saw it in great abundance, and in full flower, covering the whole inundated plain on the twelfth of October, 1815, near the ruins of Tmey, about twelve miles south-east from Mansoura, on the Damietta branch. " It dies when the water retires," (يموت لما يروح الماء) said my boatman to me.

It is therefore a fit emblem of life in all its vigour and luxuriance while it blossoms during the inundation, which is the certain cause and forerunner of plenty in Egypt. It is an emblem of death also, when quite open, as the flood then retires. Or it may be understood differently, (and I believe the Egyptians did understand it in both senses,) as indicating while in blossom that everything is covered with water, and nature, as it were, asleep; and indicating when in a state of decay that nature is restored to life, for soon after that period seeds are sown by the husbandmen—thus, inundation is life in one sense, and death in the other.

750.

ياكل و ينين

He eats and sighs.

Said of those who, in good health and prosperous circumstances, complain of sickness or murmur at fortune. ينين is used by the Egyptians for يأن " to sigh, or exclaim *Ah! Ah!*"

751.

يفتّ علي الدخان

He resembles the bread on (seeing only) the smoke.

He is preparing for some expected good fortune without any certainty of its occurring. يفتّ " to break bread into small pieces," (over which the broth is poured to make soup). The man, therefore, is said to resemble the bread in a plate when the smoke rises from the kitchen, supposing that broth is on the fire and expecting that it will be brought to him.

I happened one day in the Sinai mountains to alight at an Arab tent. Ayd, my old Bedouin guide, as soon as he had sipped his coffee, went out in search of two large stones; these he brought back to the tent, sat down, and placed them by his side. When I asked why he had done so, it appeared that his object was to use them in breaking the bones, for the sake of the marrow, of a sheep that was (as he expected) to be slaughtered in honour of us; yet he had never received the slightest intimation that such a circumstance was intended: all present began to laugh, but Ayd had not indulged a vain speculation, for soon after a copious repast of meat was placed before us.

752.

يتعلّم الحجامة في روس اليتامي

He learns cupping on the heads of orphans.

Cupping is generally applied in the East to the

hind part of the head, just above the neck. Thus in some hospitals of Europe the young surgeons learn their art by practising upon the bodies of poor patients who come to be cured *gratis*.

753.

يتعلّم البيطرة في حمير الاكراد

*He is instructed in the blacksmith's or farrier's art
(or horse-doctor's) by practising upon the asses of
the Kurds.*

This is in opposition to the proverb immediately preceding. I know not that asses are particularly esteemed by the Kurds, but this saying means that it is silly to undertake the shoeing or curing of those animals which are reckoned valuable by their owners without an adequate knowledge of the art.

754.

يوم لا هو لك لا تحسبه من عمرك

*A day that is not thine own, do not reckon it as
of thy life.*

لك "thine," "thy own." That day which thou dost not enjoy in perfect freedom ; which thou canst not pass according to thine own will.

755.

يمشي علي الحيط و يقول بالله اسلام

*He walks upon the highest part of the wall and says,
"For safety we trust to God!"*

He demands or expects safety yet does an act
which exposes him to danger. If security be thy
object do not voluntarily run into the way of danger.

756.

ينزل رجل غراب يطلع خَفّ جمل

*He descends (like) the foot of a crow, and ascends
(like) the hoof of a camel.*

Said of an ill-bred person affecting refined manners. In eating with the assistance of one's fingers
only out of the dish round which many guests are
seated, it is necessary to observe several rules of
good-breeding established among Arab gentlemen.
One rule is, to take up small morsels at a time, and
therefore to keep the fingers thrust into the dish as
close together as circumstances will allow. This
proverb is quoted in derision of an ill-bred person,
whose hand, when it descends into the dish, appears
very small to the company (as small as a crow's foot),
but when withdrawn from the dish and ascending
towards his mouth, incloses so large a piece within
its grasp that it resembles the hoof of a camel.

757.

يكذب علي الموتي و يكابر الاحيا

He tells lies of the dead and belies the living.

يكابر (from which is formed مكابرة) means in the Egyptian dialect, to affirm boldly and falsely in a person's face that he has done or said something of which he is innocent or ignorant; thus, تكابرني " dost thou belie me ? " or rather " dost thou state of me that which is a falsehood ? "

758.

يقنع من المعاصي بالتهم

He contents himself with (incurring) the suspicion of doing evil actions.

This is said of a person who does not actually commit bad actions, but constantly exposes himself to suspicion by conversing with abandoned women, associating with drunkards, men of infamous characters, &c. المعاصي means actions contrary to divine and human laws.

759.

يرمي بين الدبّ و عليقه

He causes enmity between the bear and his fodder.

He is such a mischief-maker that he sets at variance those who are most intimately united. يرمي " to throw," is often used in the sense above mentioned ; as فلان رمَى بيننا " such a person has caused mischief or enmity between us." رماني عند فلان " by calumny or false accusation he has caused such an one to become my enemy." The meddling mischief-maker bears at Cairo the appellation of نمّام

760.

ياكل ما كان و يضيِّق المكان

He eats whatever is there and contracts (or makes narrow) the place of others.

Said of a low-mannered person assuming the privileges of high rank. This proverb supposes a vulgar ill-bred man, voracious at an entertainment, (while the great Arabs never are so,) and pretending nevertheless to the privilege of a distinguished personage in occupying with his body as much room as possible, and thereby causing other guests to be crowded in their straightened places. ياكل ما كان stands for ياكل كل ما كان حاضر It is usual to say لا تضيِّق عليَّ " do not sit too close to me," or "let me have more room."

761.*

يجي زمان يترحّموا علي فرعون

A time will come when they will solicit God's mercy for Pharaoh.

Times are so bad that even Pharaoh is regretted.

The Egyptians often mention this sovereign, and the Turks call the inhabitants of Egypt by the opprobrious name of اهل فرعون or the people of Pharaoh, meaning "impious." It is said of a man who has proved stubborn, malicious, or impious, تفرعن he has become like Pharaoh.

762.

يكدّ علي عياله و يمنّ علي جيرانه

He is niggardly towards his family, but beneficent towards strangers.

يكدّ in the Egyptian dialect signifies "to curtail the dues of people," principally with respect to food. يقلل علي الطعم (See No. 748.)

763.

يخرج من الشوك ورد

A rose issues from thorns.

A good son from worthless parents.

764.

يخري في ثيابه و يقعد في الصدر متّكي

He defiles his clothes, and sits reclined in front of the company.

Of the same signification as No. 760.

The sitting rooms in Egypt are generally on such a plan as the following outlines represent :—

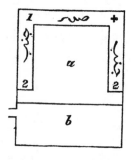

Entering the door wè find a pavement *b*, upon which the servants stand attending the company ; here the pipes and water-pots are placed. The greater portion of the room is elevated in its floor, about one foot above the pavement, and occupies the space marked *a*, on which in summer fine mats, and in winter carpets are spread. On the three sides along the walls sofas are placed even with the floor, and having numerous cushions. The sofas and divan in front of the step, or at the bottom of the room, is called "*el sader*," or the "breast." The sofas on both sides are called "*djonb*," or the "side." The place of honour is this *sader*, and especially the corner marked +, which is on the right of a person advancing towards the *sader*, wherein the great man of the company invariably takes his seat, reclining upon the cushions, while the rest, according to their rank, are ranged along the sides, and sit upon their hams, without reclining upon the cushions behind them ; that is, if they wish to pay a compli-

ment to the great man of the company. He therefore who takes his seat and reclines upon the *sader*,
either is or affects to be a man of importance.

765.

يا مشغول بهم الناس همك لمين خليته

O thou who troublest thyself about the cares of others,
to whom hast thou left thine own cares?

لمين in the Cairo pronunciation for لمَن

766.

يشتهي الحرب و يكره اللقا

He longs for war, but dislikes the battle.

لقا the meeting (of the enemy) or battle.

767.*

يا سايلي عن طعامي الخبز راس الامور

O thou who askest me about my food, (know that)
bread is the chief of all things.

Another verse of similar meaning is quoted—

القنبر قال للقيقي ما احلا التين علي الرِيقِ
قال له تاندب يا قنبر ما بعد العيش ماخبر

These lines are pronounced at Cairo as follows—

> *El kōmbar kall lil kȳky*
> *Ma ahlattyn arrȳky*
> *Kalloo tāddeb yā kōmbar*
> *Ma bād el aysh mokhabbar.*

The kombar said to the kyky, "How sweet is a fig for breakfast !"

"Learn better manners, O kombar," he replied, " after bread nothing deserves notice."

The *kombar* and *kyky* are birds about as large as sparrows, and numerous in the vicinity of Cairo. علي الريق means that state of the stomach in the morning when nothing has been swallowed except spittle, when the person is still "upon his spittle," *i.e.* with an empty stomach. التين علي الريق means "a fig upon the empty stomach," or "a fig for breakfast." The Egyptians say يفتق الريق " to breakfast," or "to eat a morsel immediately rising from bed;" which the Syrians express by يكسر الصفرة " to break the phlegm, or the bile, (by eating) or to breakfast." ما كسرت الصفرة " I have not yet breakfasted." The word ماخبر has here the sense which I have assigned to it in the above translation of the proverb; I believe it stands for ببخبر—as neither ماخبر nor ماخبر literally explained, convey in this place any true sense.

768.

يوم النصر ما فيه تعب

On the day of victory no fatigue is felt.

769.*

ينصح نصح القط للفار و الشيطان للاسان

He gives advice such as the cat gives to the mouse, or the devil to man.

Alluding to insidious advice.

770.

يبني قصرًا و يهدم مصرًا

He builds a palace and ruins a city.

This proverb is often quoted in allusion to Mohammed Aly Pasha's passion for building palaces and villas. مصر not only means Egypt or Cairo, but is also a name applied to all cities of considerable size. Thus we read in the Mohammedan law that the Friday prayer should be performed only in a city (في مصر), in opposition to the open country, of which the inhabitants, as well as all travellers, are not required to make the particular prayer of noon on Fridays. The commentators explain this term مصر as relating to any town or city governed by an emir or chief, and under the jurisdiction of a kadhy, or some head of a tribunal of justice.

771.

يقدم رجلًا و يوخر اخري

He advances one leg and draws back the other.

He wants decision and is unstable in all his actions.

772.

يُلْجِم الفار في بيته

The mouse is bridled in his house.

Said of a miser in whose house even the mouse
has been bridled, lest it should be able to eat anything.

773.

يا والي لا تجور الولاية لا تدوم

*O governor do not tyrannize—the dominion does not
'last for ever.*

774.

يسبّح تسبيح الفار سبحان مَن خلقني للفساد

*He prays upon his rosary the prayer of the mouse,
"O most holy, who hast created me for vile doings."*

Said of base hypocrites who are constantly seen
with rosaries in their hands. The word سبحان is
repeated during prayer thirty-three times in passing
so many beads through the fingers, and expresses
that God is free from all defects or faults, and most
pure and holy.

775.

يلطم وجهي و يقول ليش هذا يبكي

He strikes my face, and says "Why does this man cry?"

On the unjust ruler, who expresses surprise at the complaints of his subjects. لِي شي for ليش

776.

يقول للسارق اسرق و لصاحب المنزل احفظ متاعك

He says to the thief, "Steal;" and to the house-owner, "Take care of thy goods."

Applied to double-dealers.

777.

يفتي علي الابرة و يبلع المدرة

He pronounces judgment upon a needle, and (at the same time) swallows a large pole.

He is rigid in judging the affairs of others, but commits flagrant peculation himself. يبلع is used like اكل to signify that a person devours property not his own nor confided to his care. مدرة signifies in Egypt the long pole with which sailors push on the vessels in shallow water.

778.

يمينك ما تدري عن شمالك

Thy right hand knows nothing of thy left hand.

Mohammed has taken this principle from the Scripture. One of his sayings is recorded which concludes with the following words—

رجل تصدّق بصدقة فلم تعلم شماله ما انفقت يمينه

A man distributes alms, and his left hand does not know what his right hand dispenses.

779.

يدلّل العبد و يضربه

He spoils the slave and then beats him.

Said of those who spoil their inferiors or their children, and then punish them for what their own folly has caused. دلّل in the Egyptian dialect "to spoil (a child) by too much indulgence;" for يدلّل we often hear يدلّع

780.

ياكل و يتنقور

He eats and (at the same time) mocks (at what he eats).

Instead of thanking, he ridicules the host. يتنقور is a low word of the Egyptian dialect synonymous with يتمسخر

781.

يوم في العافية كثير

One day in (perfect) health is much.

العافية is the most common salutation which one receives on the road from peasants ; they pronounce it " *Howáfye.*" The reply is الله يعانيك

782.

يري الشاهد ما لا يري الغايب

The eye-witness observes what the absent does not see.

THE END.

A CATALOG OF SELECTED
DOVER BOOKS
IN ALL FIELDS OF INTEREST

A CATALOG OF SELECTED DOVER
BOOKS IN ALL FIELDS OF INTEREST

CONCERNING THE SPIRITUAL IN ART, Wassily Kandinsky. Pioneering work by father of abstract art. Thoughts on color theory, nature of art. Analysis of earlier masters. 12 illustrations. 80pp. of text. 5⅜ x 8½. 23411-8

ANIMALS: 1,419 Copyright-Free Illustrations of Mammals, Birds, Fish, Insects, etc., Jim Harter (ed.). Clear wood engravings present, in extremely lifelike poses, over 1,000 species of animals. One of the most extensive pictorial sourcebooks of its kind. Captions. Index. 284pp. 9 x 12. 23766-4

CELTIC ART: The Methods of Construction, George Bain. Simple geometric techniques for making Celtic interlacements, spirals, Kells-type initials, animals, humans, etc. Over 500 illustrations. 160pp. 9 x 12. (Available in U.S. only.) 22923-8

AN ATLAS OF ANATOMY FOR ARTISTS, Fritz Schider. Most thorough reference work on art anatomy in the world. Hundreds of illustrations, including selections from works by Vesalius, Leonardo, Goya, Ingres, Michelangelo, others. 593 illustrations. 192pp. 7⅛ x 10¼. 20241-0

CELTIC HAND STROKE-BY-STROKE (Irish Half-Uncial from "The Book of Kells"): An Arthur Baker Calligraphy Manual, Arthur Baker. Complete guide to creating each letter of the alphabet in distinctive Celtic manner. Covers hand position, strokes, pens, inks, paper, more. Illustrated. 48pp. 8¼ x 11. 24336-2

EASY ORIGAMI, John Montroll. Charming collection of 32 projects (hat, cup, pelican, piano, swan, many more) specially designed for the novice origami hobbyist. Clearly illustrated easy-to-follow instructions insure that even beginning papercrafters will achieve successful results. 48pp. 8¼ x 11. 27298-2

THE COMPLETE BOOK OF BIRDHOUSE CONSTRUCTION FOR WOODWORKERS, Scott D. Campbell. Detailed instructions, illustrations, tables. Also data on bird habitat and instinct patterns. Bibliography. 3 tables. 63 illustrations in 15 figures. 48pp. 5¼ x 8½. 24407-5

BLOOMINGDALE'S ILLUSTRATED 1886 CATALOG: Fashions, Dry Goods and Housewares, Bloomingdale Brothers. Famed merchants' extremely rare catalog depicting about 1,700 products: clothing, housewares, firearms, dry goods, jewelry, more. Invaluable for dating, identifying vintage items. Also, copyright-free graphics for artists, designers. Co-published with Henry Ford Museum & Greenfield Village. 160pp. 8¼ x 11. 25780-0

HISTORIC COSTUME IN PICTURES, Braun & Schneider. Over 1,450 costumed figures in clearly detailed engravings–from dawn of civilization to end of 19th century. Captions. Many folk costumes. 256pp. 8⅜ x 11¾. 23150-X

THE CLARINET AND CLARINET PLAYING, David Pino. Lively, comprehensive work features suggestions about technique, musicianship, and musical interpretation, as well as guidelines for teaching, making your own reeds, and preparing for public performance. Includes an intriguing look at clarinet history. "A godsend," *The Clarinet*, Journal of the International Clarinet Society. Appendixes. 7 illus. 320pp. 5⅜ x 8½. 40270-3

HOLLYWOOD GLAMOR PORTRAITS, John Kobal (ed.). 145 photos from 1926-49. Harlow, Gable, Bogart, Bacall; 94 stars in all. Full background on photographers, technical aspects. 160pp. 8⅜ x 11¼. 23352-9

THE ANNOTATED CASEY AT THE BAT: A Collection of Ballads about the Mighty Casey/Third, Revised Edition, Martin Gardner (ed.). Amusing sequels and parodies of one of America's best-loved poems: Casey's Revenge, Why Casey Whiffed, Casey's Sister at the Bat, others. 256pp. 5⅜ x 8½. 28598-7

THE RAVEN AND OTHER FAVORITE POEMS, Edgar Allan Poe. Over 40 of the author's most memorable poems: "The Bells," "Ulalume," "Israfel," "To Helen," "The Conqueror Worm," "Eldorado," "Annabel Lee," many more. Alphabetic lists of titles and first lines. 64pp. 5$\frac{3}{16}$ x 8¼. 26685-0

PERSONAL MEMOIRS OF U. S. GRANT, Ulysses Simpson Grant. Intelligent, deeply moving firsthand account of Civil War campaigns, considered by many the finest military memoirs ever written. Includes letters, historic photographs, maps and more. 528pp. 6⅛ x 9¼. 28587-1

ANCIENT EGYPTIAN MATERIALS AND INDUSTRIES, A. Lucas and J. Harris. Fascinating, comprehensive, thoroughly documented text describes this ancient civilization's vast resources and the processes that incorporated them in daily life, including the use of animal products, building materials, cosmetics, perfumes and incense, fibers, glazed ware, glass and its manufacture, materials used in the mummification process, and much more. 544pp. 6⅛ x 9¼. (Available in U.S. only.) 40446-3

RUSSIAN STORIES/RUSSKIE RASSKAZY: A Dual-Language Book, edited by Gleb Struve. Twelve tales by such masters as Chekhov, Tolstoy, Dostoevsky, Pushkin, others. Excellent word-for-word English translations on facing pages, plus teaching and study aids, Russian/English vocabulary, biographical/critical introductions, more. 416pp. 5⅜ x 8½. 26244-8

PHILADELPHIA THEN AND NOW: 60 Sites Photographed in the Past and Present, Kenneth Finkel and Susan Oyama. Rare photographs of City Hall, Logan Square, Independence Hall, Betsy Ross House, other landmarks juxtaposed with contemporary views. Captures changing face of historic city. Introduction. Captions. 128pp. 8¼ x 11. 25790-8

AIA ARCHITECTURAL GUIDE TO NASSAU AND SUFFOLK COUNTIES, LONG ISLAND, The American Institute of Architects, Long Island Chapter, and the Society for the Preservation of Long Island Antiquities. Comprehensive, well-researched and generously illustrated volume brings to life over three centuries of Long Island's great architectural heritage. More than 240 photographs with authoritative, extensively detailed captions. 176pp. 8¼ x 11. 26946-9

NORTH AMERICAN INDIAN LIFE: Customs and Traditions of 23 Tribes, Elsie Clews Parsons (ed.). 27 fictionalized essays by noted anthropologists examine religion, customs, government, additional facets of life among the Winnebago, Crow, Zuni, Eskimo, other tribes. 480pp. 6⅛ x 9¼. 27377-6

MY BONDAGE AND MY FREEDOM, Frederick Douglass. Born a slave, Douglass became outspoken force in antislavery movement. The best of Douglass' autobiographies. Graphic description of slave life. 464pp. 5⅜ x 8½.   22457-0

FOLLOWING THE EQUATOR: A Journey Around the World, Mark Twain. Fascinating humorous account of 1897 voyage to Hawaii, Australia, India, New Zealand, etc. Ironic, bemused reports on peoples, customs, climate, flora and fauna, politics, much more. 197 illustrations. 720pp. 5⅜ x 8½.   26113-1

THE PEOPLE CALLED SHAKERS, Edward D. Andrews. Definitive study of Shakers: origins, beliefs, practices, dances, social organization, furniture and crafts, etc. 33 illustrations. 351pp. 5⅜ x 8½.   21081-2

THE MYTHS OF GREECE AND ROME, H. A. Guerber. A classic of mythology, generously illustrated, long prized for its simple, graphic, accurate retelling of the principal myths of Greece and Rome, and for its commentary on their origins and significance. With 64 illustrations by Michelangelo, Raphael, Titian, Rubens, Canova, Bernini and others. 480pp. 5⅜ x 8½.   27584-1

PSYCHOLOGY OF MUSIC, Carl E. Seashore. Classic work discusses music as a medium from psychological viewpoint. Clear treatment of physical acoustics, auditory apparatus, sound perception, development of musical skills, nature of musical feeling, host of other topics. 88 figures. 408pp. 5⅜ x 8½.   21851-1

THE PHILOSOPHY OF HISTORY, Georg W. Hegel. Great classic of Western thought develops concept that history is not chance but rational process, the evolution of freedom. 457pp. 5⅜ x 8½.   20112-0

THE BOOK OF TEA, Kakuzo Okakura. Minor classic of the Orient: entertaining, charming explanation, interpretation of traditional Japanese culture in terms of tea ceremony. 94pp. 5⅜ x 8½.   20070-1

LIFE IN ANCIENT EGYPT, Adolf Erman. Fullest, most thorough, detailed older account with much not in more recent books, domestic life, religion, magic, medicine, commerce, much more. Many illustrations reproduce tomb paintings, carvings, hieroglyphs, etc. 597pp. 5⅜ x 8½.   22632-8

SUNDIALS, Their Theory and Construction, Albert Waugh. Far and away the best, most thorough coverage of ideas, mathematics concerned, types, construction, adjusting anywhere. Simple, nontechnical treatment allows even children to build several of these dials. Over 100 illustrations. 230pp. 5⅜ x 8½.   22947-5

THEORETICAL HYDRODYNAMICS, L. M. Milne-Thomson. Classic exposition of the mathematical theory of fluid motion, applicable to both hydrodynamics and aerodynamics. Over 600 exercises. 768pp. 6⅛ x 9¼.   68970-0

SONGS OF EXPERIENCE: Facsimile Reproduction with 26 Plates in Full Color, William Blake. 26 full-color plates from a rare 1826 edition. Includes "The Tyger," "London," "Holy Thursday," and other poems. Printed text of poems. 48pp. 5¼ x 7.
                                                                                        24636-1

OLD-TIME VIGNETTES IN FULL COLOR, Carol Belanger Grafton (ed.). Over 390 charming, often sentimental illustrations, selected from archives of Victorian graphics—pretty women posing, children playing, food, flowers, kittens and puppies, smiling cherubs, birds and butterflies, much more. All copyright-free. 48pp. 9¼ x 12¼.
                                                                                        27269-9

PIANO TUNING, J. Cree Fischer. Clearest, best book for beginner, amateur. Simple repairs, raising dropped notes, tuning by easy method of flattened fifths. No previous skills needed. 4 illustrations. 201pp. 5⅜ x 8½. 23267-0

HINTS TO SINGERS, Lillian Nordica. Selecting the right teacher, developing confidence, overcoming stage fright, and many other important skills receive thoughtful discussion in this indispensible guide, written by a world-famous diva of four decades' experience. 96pp. 5⅜ x 8½. 40094-8

THE COMPLETE NONSENSE OF EDWARD LEAR, Edward Lear. All nonsense limericks, zany alphabets, Owl and Pussycat, songs, nonsense botany, etc., illustrated by Lear. Total of 320pp. 5⅜ x 8½. (Available in U.S. only.) 20167-8

VICTORIAN PARLOUR POETRY: An Annotated Anthology, Michael R. Turner. 117 gems by Longfellow, Tennyson, Browning, many lesser-known poets. "The Village Blacksmith," "Curfew Must Not Ring Tonight," "Only a Baby Small," dozens more, often difficult to find elsewhere. Index of poets, titles, first lines. xxiii + 325pp. 5⅜ x 8¼. 27044-0

DUBLINERS, James Joyce. Fifteen stories offer vivid, tightly focused observations of the lives of Dublin's poorer classes. At least one, "The Dead," is considered a masterpiece. Reprinted complete and unabridged from standard edition. 160pp. 5³⁄₁₆ x 8¼. 26870-5

GREAT WEIRD TALES: 14 Stories by Lovecraft, Blackwood, Machen and Others, S. T. Joshi (ed.). 14 spellbinding tales, including "The Sin Eater," by Fiona McLeod, "The Eye Above the Mantel," by Frank Belknap Long, as well as renowned works by R. H. Barlow, Lord Dunsany, Arthur Machen, W. C. Morrow and eight other masters of the genre. 256pp. 5⅜ x 8½. (Available in U.S. only.) 40436-6

THE BOOK OF THE SACRED MAGIC OF ABRAMELIN THE MAGE, translated by S. MacGregor Mathers. Medieval manuscript of ceremonial magic. Basic document in Aleister Crowley, Golden Dawn groups. 268pp. 5⅜ x 8½. 23211-5

NEW RUSSIAN-ENGLISH AND ENGLISH-RUSSIAN DICTIONARY, M. A. O'Brien. This is a remarkably handy Russian dictionary, containing a surprising amount of information, including over 70,000 entries. 366pp. 4½ x 6⅛. 20208-9

HISTORIC HOMES OF THE AMERICAN PRESIDENTS, Second, Revised Edition, Irvin Haas. A traveler's guide to American Presidential homes, most open to the public, depicting and describing homes occupied by every American President from George Washington to George Bush. With visiting hours, admission charges, travel routes. 175 photographs. Index. 160pp. 8¼ x 11. 26751-2

NEW YORK IN THE FORTIES, Andreas Feininger. 162 brilliant photographs by the well-known photographer, formerly with *Life* magazine. Commuters, shoppers, Times Square at night, much else from city at its peak. Captions by John von Hartz. 181pp. 9¼ x 10¾. 23585-8

INDIAN SIGN LANGUAGE, William Tomkins. Over 525 signs developed by Sioux and other tribes. Written instructions and diagrams. Also 290 pictographs. 111pp. 6⅛ x 9¼. 22029-X

THE WIT AND HUMOR OF OSCAR WILDE, Alvin Redman (ed.). More than 1,000 ripostes, paradoxes, wisecracks: Work is the curse of the drinking classes; I can resist everything except temptation; etc. 258pp. 5⅜ x 8½. 20602-5

SHAKESPEARE LEXICON AND QUOTATION DICTIONARY, Alexander Schmidt. Full definitions, locations, shades of meaning in every word in plays and poems. More than 50,000 exact quotations. 1,485pp. 6½ x 9¼. 2-vol. set.
Vol. 1: 22726-X
Vol. 2: 22727-8

SELECTED POEMS, Emily Dickinson. Over 100 best-known, best-loved poems by one of America's foremost poets, reprinted from authoritative early editions. No comparable edition at this price. Index of first lines. 64pp. 5 3/16 x 8¼. 26466-1

THE INSIDIOUS DR. FU-MANCHU, Sax Rohmer. The first of the popular mystery series introduces a pair of English detectives to their archnemesis, the diabolical Dr. Fu-Manchu. Flavorful atmosphere, fast-paced action, and colorful characters enliven this classic of the genre. 208pp. 5 3/16 x 8¼. 29898-1

THE MALLEUS MALEFICARUM OF KRAMER AND SPRENGER, translated by Montague Summers. Full text of most important witchhunter's "bible," used by both Catholics and Protestants. 278pp. 6⅝ x 10. 22802-9

SPANISH STORIES/CUENTOS ESPAÑOLES: A Dual-Language Book, Angel Flores (ed.). Unique format offers 13 great stories in Spanish by Cervantes, Borges, others. Faithful English translations on facing pages. 352pp. 5⅜ x 8½. 25399-6

GARDEN CITY, LONG ISLAND, IN EARLY PHOTOGRAPHS, 1869–1919, Mildred H. Smith. Handsome treasury of 118 vintage pictures, accompanied by carefully researched captions, document the Garden City Hotel fire (1899), the Vanderbilt Cup Race (1908), the first airmail flight departing from the Nassau Boulevard Aerodrome (1911), and much more. 96pp. 8⅞ x 11¾. 40669-5

OLD QUEENS, N.Y., IN EARLY PHOTOGRAPHS, Vincent F. Seyfried and William Asadorian. Over 160 rare photographs of Maspeth, Jamaica, Jackson Heights, and other areas. Vintage views of DeWitt Clinton mansion, 1939 World's Fair and more. Captions. 192pp. 8⅞ x 11. 26358-4

CAPTURED BY THE INDIANS: 15 Firsthand Accounts, 1750-1870, Frederick Drimmer. Astounding true historical accounts of grisly torture, bloody conflicts, relentless pursuits, miraculous escapes and more, by people who lived to tell the tale. 384pp. 5⅜ x 8½. 24901-8

THE WORLD'S GREAT SPEECHES (Fourth Enlarged Edition), Lewis Copeland, Lawrence W. Lamm, and Stephen J. McKenna. Nearly 300 speeches provide public speakers with a wealth of updated quotes and inspiration–from Pericles' funeral oration and William Jennings Bryan's "Cross of Gold Speech" to Malcolm X's powerful words on the Black Revolution and Earl of Spenser's tribute to his sister, Diana, Princess of Wales. 944pp. 5⅜ x 8⅜. 40903-1

THE BOOK OF THE SWORD, Sir Richard F. Burton. Great Victorian scholar/adventurer's eloquent, erudite history of the "queen of weapons"–from prehistory to early Roman Empire. Evolution and development of early swords, variations (sabre, broadsword, cutlass, scimitar, etc.), much more. 336pp. 6⅛ x 9¼.
25434-8

THE STORY OF THE TITANIC AS TOLD BY ITS SURVIVORS, Jack Winocour (ed.). What it was really like. Panic, despair, shocking inefficiency, and a little heroism. More thrilling than any fictional account. 26 illustrations. 320pp. 5⅜ x 8½.
20610-6

FAIRY AND FOLK TALES OF THE IRISH PEASANTRY, William Butler Yeats (ed.). Treasury of 64 tales from the twilight world of Celtic myth and legend: "The Soul Cages," "The Kildare Pooka," "King O'Toole and his Goose," many more. Introduction and Notes by W. B. Yeats. 352pp. 5⅜ x 8½.
26941-8

BUDDHIST MAHAYANA TEXTS, E. B. Cowell and others (eds.). Superb, accurate translations of basic documents in Mahayana Buddhism, highly important in history of religions. The Buddha-karita of Asvaghosha, Larger Sukhavativyuha, more. 448pp. 5⅜ x 8½.
25552-2

ONE TWO THREE . . . INFINITY: Facts and Speculations of Science, George Gamow. Great physicist's fascinating, readable overview of contemporary science: number theory, relativity, fourth dimension, entropy, genes, atomic structure, much more. 128 illustrations. Index. 352pp. 5⅜ x 8½.
25664-2

EXPERIMENTATION AND MEASUREMENT, W. J. Youden. Introductory manual explains laws of measurement in simple terms and offers tips for achieving accuracy and minimizing errors. Mathematics of measurement, use of instruments, experimenting with machines. 1994 edition. Foreword. Preface. Introduction. Epilogue. Selected Readings. Glossary. Index. Tables and figures. 128pp. 5⅜ x 8½.
40451-X

DALÍ ON MODERN ART: The Cuckolds of Antiquated Modern Art, Salvador Dalí. Influential painter skewers modern art and its practitioners. Outrageous evaluations of Picasso, Cézanne, Turner, more. 15 renderings of paintings discussed. 44 calligraphic decorations by Dalí. 96pp. 5⅜ x 8½. (Available in U.S. only.)
29220-7

ANTIQUE PLAYING CARDS: A Pictorial History, Henry René D'Allemagne. Over 900 elaborate, decorative images from rare playing cards (14th–20th centuries): Bacchus, death, dancing dogs, hunting scenes, royal coats of arms, players cheating, much more. 96pp. 9¼ x 12¼.
29265-7

MAKING FURNITURE MASTERPIECES: 30 Projects with Measured Drawings, Franklin H. Gottshall. Step-by-step instructions, illustrations for constructing handsome, useful pieces, among them a Sheraton desk, Chippendale chair, Spanish desk, Queen Anne table and a William and Mary dressing mirror. 224pp. 8⅛ x 11¼.
29338-6

THE FOSSIL BOOK: A Record of Prehistoric Life, Patricia V. Rich et al. Profusely illustrated definitive guide covers everything from single-celled organisms and dinosaurs to birds and mammals and the interplay between climate and man. Over 1,500 illustrations. 760pp. 7½ x 10⅛.
29371-8

Paperbound unless otherwise indicated. Available at your book dealer, online at **www.doverpublications.com**, or by writing to Dept. GI, Dover Publications, Inc., 31 East 2nd Street, Mineola, NY 11501. For current price information or for free catalogues (please indicate field of interest), write to Dover Publications or log on to **www.doverpublications.com** and see every Dover book in print. Dover publishes more than 500 books each year on science, elementary and advanced mathematics, biology, music, art, literary history, social sciences, and other areas.